"Sue Roffey has written an essential bc[...]e globe. The ASPIRE principles encompass foundational pilla[...]arning and well-being for all children and youth. This is a user-friendly volume with many practical applications. Teachers and educational administrators around the world will benefit greatly from the wisdom in these pages. I highly recommend it to educators, parents, psychologists, counsellors, and anyone interested in flourishing and the creation of a just and vibrant society."

Isaac Prilleltensky, *Professor, PhD, University of Miami*

"As Sue Roffey articulates so intelligently, passionately and clearly, wellbeing is both complex and contextual. This book provides a comprehensive and clear framework for considering how best to grow contextual wellbeing across your whole school using her well established ASPIRE principles. A fabulous foundation for whole-school development, and a much-needed voice for wellbeing equity."

Helen Street, *Founder of Contextual Wellbeing and Positive Schools, Honorary Fellow, The University of Western Australia*

"This excellent book shows how to enable pupils to flourish in school now and how we can help all to thrive in future. The ASPIRE principles build social justice. I highly recommend it."

Anthony Seldon, *Co-chair of the* Times Education Commission Report: Bringing out the Best

"Wellbeing is not merely a means to an end. It is the end goal we all aspire to, and how ultimately, we measure the success of our lives. Dr Sue Roffey's ASPIRE books provide a pathway for schools to build wellbeing for all – students, educators, and community. Dr Roffey illustrates how the ASPIRE principles can underpin the values of a school, inform and drive policy, practice and structure, and guide teacher-student relationships. This work is pro-active, comprehensive and universal and aims at nothing less than a revitalisation of education."

Denise Quinlan, *Director of the New Zealand Institute of Wellbeing and Resilience*

"I have no hesitation in recommending this book to all educators – wellbeing and learning must be a focus for us all if we are to build successful schools and more importantly successful families of the future. Sue's ASPIRE framework provides us with a clear structure to frame our thinking."

Maureen McKenna, *Former Executive Director of Education, City of Glasgow*

"For true educational change we need to know to what we aspire. Drawing from both her rich experience and the best educational science, Roffey points us toward educational contexts in which students want to learn. She points us beyond a narrow focus on cognitive achievement, to the kind of schools where human development, intellectual, social, and emotional, is the goal. Beyond piecemeal reform she describes cultures of education where both students and teachers can flourish. This is a book that can truly lead the way of positive school change."

Richard M. Ryan, *Professor, Institute for Positive Psychology and Education, Australian Catholic University, North Sydney and Distinguished Professor, College of Education, Ewha Womans University, South Korea*

"There has been some talk post pandemic of doing things differently in schools and not just returning to default settings in search of a more rewarding and compelling school vision for educators and students. This inspiring and thoughtful book provides the narrative for this work. It poses the question, does the education system as we know it meet the needs of learners and educators or is there another way? A way which provides the skills that employers want, the happiness that parents seek for their children and a way of teaching and learning which helps to retain and recruit those who work in our schools. Sue's book covers key aspects of what an education system fit for the 21st century must include."

Andy Mellor, *National Wellbeing Director for Schools Advisory Service,*
National Association of Head Teachers National President 18/19,
Strategic Lead for Carnegie centre of excellence for mental health in schools.

"Sue's aspirations and vision for a truly inclusive, critical, and hopeful approach to education is one that is sorely needed. Sue's work guides schools, educators, and psychologists to see wellbeing as something to be actively pursued and cultivated, rather than just the absence of mental ill-health. The realisation of the ASPIRE principles would mark a systems change in how we 'do' education."

Dan O'Hare, *Educational Psychologist, Senior Lecturer,*
University of Bristol and founder of edpsy.org.uk

"As educators and educational leaders, we continually seek pathways to profoundly impact generations of learners. Dr Roffey's work is a vital contribution to this journey, offering both inspiration and practical strategies for creating educational environments where every child can flourish. This book presents a transformative vision for education, deeply resonating with the Global Citizenship Foundation's mandate to transform education for human and planetary flourishing. I hope this essential resource reaches practitioners and policymakers committed to nurturing inclusive, sustainable, and equitable environments where every child can realize their full potential and flourish."

Aaryan Salman, *Director-General, Global Citizenship Foundation, India*

"As we enter a more and more tumultuous century, we and our children will have to master social/political and climate challenges as well as disinformation. Sue Roffey, in her passionately argued and practical book, shows us the way. Based on her vast experience in positive education, she describes how children, educators and larger society may achieve greater wellbeing and resilience through a shared learning environment. In her ASPIRE program, she elaborates the basic elements for transforming today's education systems, and indeed our lives, into one that allows the development of thriving children. An important read!"

Marten W. de Vries, *Emeritus Professor, Social Psychiatry and*
Public Mental Health, Maastricht University, Netherlands; Chair,
Mind Venture International Institute; Knighted in the Order of the Dutch Lion

"Sue Roffey is a force of nature and this book is everything you would expect: intelligent, insightful and driven by a burning sense of social justice. The question of what education is for is too often overlooked. The consequences are clear: the wellbeing of educators, as well as children and young people, is not in good shape. Research-informed, humane and practical, the ASPIRE model is the antidote we so badly need. Despite the name, this is not aspirational stuff. It is urgent reading that should rocket to the top of every educator's reading pile. Grab it with both hands and implement it in your schools. Your colleagues, pupils and their families will thank you for it for many years to come."

James Mannion, *Director, Rethinking Education; Co-author,* Fear is the Mind Killer

ASPIRE to Wellbeing and Learning for All in Secondary Settings

This truly accessible resource shows secondary school practitioners how to help make every child and young person feel like they really matter when they are in school, so they can develop confidence, resilience, love of learning, a positive sense of self, and healthy relationships.

Sue Roffey shows how to create a learning environment where all pupils can thrive and make progress in learning and where wellbeing for everyone is at the heart of every school. By using the unique evidence-based ASPIRE principles of Agency, Safety, Positivity, Inclusion, Respect, and Equity in practice, this insightful book shows teachers how to redress the balance in ways that maximise a love for learning, build a positive sense of self, construct healthy relationships, foster resilience, and help young people make good choices. This resource features a chapter for each principle which explores *what* this means, *why* it matters, and *how* it can be applied across secondary schools. Although visionary, the book is based on both substantial evidence and good practice, with each chapter supported by case studies across the world.

The book demonstrates the positive difference each principle makes to children in primary school settings as well as to teachers, parents, and the overall community. It is a must-read for secondary school teachers, tutors, school leaders, psychologists, parents, and anyone who wants an education system that is inclusive, holistic, and effective for all students.

Sue Roffey is a teacher, psychologist, academic, author, speaker, and social activist. She is also Honorary Associate Professor at University College London, UK, and Director of Growing Great Schools Worldwide. She has previously published *Creating the World We Want to Live in* (Routledge, 2021), *The Primary Behaviour Cookbook* (Routledge, 2018), and *The Secondary Behaviour Cookbook* (Routledge, 2018).

ASPIRE to Wellbeing and Learning for All in Secondary Settings

The Principles Underpinning Positive Education

Sue Roffey

Routledge
Taylor & Francis Group

LONDON AND NEW YORK

First published 2025
by Routledge
4 Park Square, Milton Park, Abingdon, Oxon OX14 4RN

and by Routledge
605 Third Avenue, New York, NY 10158

Routledge is an imprint of the Taylor & Francis Group, an informa business

© 2025 Sue Roffey

The right of Sue Roffey to be identified as author of this work has been asserted in accordance with sections 77 and 78 of the Copyright, Designs and Patents Act 1988.

All rights reserved. No part of this book may be reprinted or reproduced or utilised in any form or by any electronic, mechanical, or other means, now known or hereafter invented, including photocopying and recording, or in any information storage or retrieval system, without permission in writing from the publishers.

Trademark notice: Product or corporate names may be trademarks or registered trademarks, and are used only for identification and explanation without intent to infringe.

British Library Cataloguing-in-Publication Data
A catalogue record for this book is available from the British Library

ISBN: 978-1-032-54952-1 (hbk)
ISBN: 978-1-032-54951-4 (pbk)
ISBN: 978-1-003-42824-4 (ebk)

DOI: 10.4324/9781003428244

Typeset in Galliard
by SPi Technologies India Pvt Ltd (Straive)

This book is dedicated to all those teachers who, beyond academics, believe in the best of young people and change their lives for the better.

Contents

Acknowledgements

It has taken well over a decade to develop ASPIRE. During that time, I have worked with schools, educators, researchers, families and communities, children and young people in many countries. For the most part, they have deepened my belief in humanity and that people want the best for young people and their future. Some have needed courage in the face of opposition from policy makers and others who have a vision for education that is not about wellbeing and learning for all, but about social control or building a business. I have learnt so much from them which has confirmed the validity and value of ASPIRE, not only in education but also in relationships – at home, at work, and in our communities.

It is difficult to name everyone in this venture, but there are those without whom this book would not have seen the light of day. Foremost is my husband David: proof-reader, formatter, reference checker, indexer, techno adviser, tea-maker, comforter, and travel agent. His support is integral to my own wellbeing, my thinking, and my work. The rest of my family and close friends also deserve a mention as they keep me both grounded and uplifted!

Routledge Education are brilliant to work with, and Alison Foyle, who has commissioned several of my books, is a star. Her belief in me and my approach to education has been a constant in this endeavour. I am immensely grateful.

I would like to also express my deep thanks for the willingness of so many to write about their experiences to illustrate the value of the principles. This is the strength of the book – being able to visualise examples of good practice throughout. All the ASPIRE principles are based in academic evidence, but they are brought alive by the stories that powerfully illustrate the difference they make to young people, their teachers, and the future.

Sue Roffey
January 2024

Introduction

This book addresses three interlinked questions:

- What is education for?
- What do we want for our learners in school now?
- What sort of society do we want them to live in – and contribute to?

Do we want young people to be curious about the world around them, excited by new discoveries, fascinated by all the possibilities for learning and keen to explore further, or do we just want them to get through the curriculum and cause as little trouble as possible? Of course, all students need to learn the basics in order to function in today's world, but there are ways to do this that promote an innate love of learning rather than stifle it.

Do we want a society that maximises the potential of all citizens and ensures that everyone has what they need for optimal mental and physical health, and to live life with meaning, purpose and engagement? Or are we prepared to put up with increasing inequality, escalating unhappiness, deteriorating mental health, rising crime, misogyny, racism and corruption? If we want values of kindness, inclusion, fairness, and respect for all to feature in our communities, what happens in education is critical.

Education is a means of preparing every individual for the challenges of the 21st century, showing them how to engage fully with learning about the world around them and discriminate between what is real and what is not. Do we want students to have respect for science and evidence and be uplifted by creativity and innovation, or is education just a means to an economic end? Is education about the freedom for each student to become the best they can be or a means of social control? These are rarely absolutes, but the questions are relevant.

People talk about 'raising standards' in education as if the definition of education were a given. There is less discussion about 'raising engagement', let alone joy in learning. Education matters: what pupils are taught, how they are taught, and their experiences of the learning environment. School is where students discover all the possibilities of knowledge and understanding as well as who they can become. It is where they have the possibility of learning how to build the relationships for individuals, families and communities to thrive. In some countries this is happening. In others it is not, and the outcomes are seen in disaffection, disengagement, and despair for some and perhaps privilege for others … but not necessarily good mental health and a life well lived.

This book's title – *Wellbeing and Learning for All* – emphasises social justice. We are concerned about what is happening for all students in schools here and now, but also the future we are creating. What young people learn, both within and beyond the curriculum, shapes our world.

DOI: 10.4324/9781003428244-1

Beyond the pandemic

Covid-19 has had a profound impact on young people and their learning across the world. It has increased inequalities everywhere and also highlighted many issues in education. Some students felt safer and happier at home, away from academic pressure, bullying and comparison with others: others became more vulnerable, as they were no longer monitored in a school setting. Although there was often the option of online learning, a concern for many was disconnection from their peers, especially for adolescents. Feeling you belong is a cornerstone of resilience and for teenagers is also related to the development of identity. Mental health has further deteriorated, and attendance in school has not returned to previous levels. There has been a 'catch-up' push from governments, but many organisations and educators have said that social and emotional wellbeing has to be a priority if students are to progress with learning. The impact of the pandemic may potentially affect a generation, especially for those already disadvantaged. This makes it even more vital that education be well resourced; learners feel welcomed, valued, connected, and accepted for who they are; the curriculum is relevant and meaningful; and school is a place where students want to be.

Positive psychology

Traditional psychology aims to identify and analyse problems, with a view to developing effective treatments and interventions. Although there will always be a need for this, positive psychology has a different focus, in that it seeks pro-active solutions that enable people to flourish and thrive. Rather than look for what is wrong and how can we fix it, positive psychology asks: "*What do we know helps people become the best of themselves?*", "*How can we enable people to cope with the challenges life throws at them*", "*What skills and attitudes promote authentic wellbeing?*", and "*What needs to happen so everyone has a chance of living well and contributing to the wellbeing of others?*"

Positive education

Positive education emerged from the study of positive psychology and puts equal emphasis on wellbeing and learning – making connections between the two. Students make more progress in learning when they are experiencing a safe and inclusive school environment, and feeling good about themselves and their progress, other people, and what is happening around them. This is not just about pupils, but also teachers, families and communities. Throughout the book we address the following:

- What would we see and hear in a healthy learning environment?
- What is already going well in terms of all young people enjoying learning, feeling connected and making progress, and how might we get more of this?
- How can we align what happens in schools with what promotes healthy child and adolescent development? This includes intrinsic motivation, a positive self-concept, and opportunities to explore, experiment, be creative and be challenged.
- What enables educators to be valued and respected for the vital roles they fulfil?
- How can education systems promote the perceptions and competencies that enable young people to flourish?
- What will ensure that young people of all abilities and from all communities, backgrounds and circumstances have both the educational approaches and resources they need to learn and thrive in education?

Wellbeing

Wellbeing is both complex and contextual (Street, 2018). It underpins not only mental health, but also engagement with learning. The higher the level of wellbeing across a school, the more resilient the pupils, the more pro-social the behaviour, the greater the engagement of pupils, the better their achievements and the more teacher satisfaction (Noble et al., 2008).

Although many schools are doing their best, too many students, alongside teachers, are not having a good time in education. Wellbeing is still often reactive and takes place in silos rather than being pro-active, comprehensive and universal – what happens for everyone, every day. This book aims to maximise a love for learning, build a positive sense of self, construct healthy relationships, foster resilience, and help young people and educators make good choices. It also embraces the wellbeing of teachers and relationships with communities.

There are many excellent texts on wellbeing and positive education, but for the most part they address issues separately such as leadership, teacher wellbeing and behaviour. This book takes a different direction, and instead talks about how each of the ASPIRE principles needs to be embedded through everything that happens in a school.

Learning for all

Though not acknowledged by every country, education has been recognised as a human right for all children across the world since 1948 (UNICEF, 2007). This is encapsulated in the United Nations Convention on the Rights of the Child (UNCROC), Article 28:

> *Every child has the right to an education. Primary education must be free and different forms of secondary education must be available to every child.*

There are references to other articles in UNCROC throughout the book, confirming that ASPIRE is integral to children's rights and how they should be treated in all circumstances, including in education.

There is significant evidence that the principles of ASPIRE impact positively on learning itself. The following is a quote from the UK Department for Education (Greatbatch & Tate, 2019):

> **Factors associated with countries high-performing education systems:** *Although a disparate array of factors is associated with the high performance of education systems in Estonia, Finland, Germany, Singapore and Taiwan, there are some common factors between these countries. These include: high levels of equity in educational outcomes/achievement (Estonia and Finland), teacher-quality (Finland and Singapore), support for pupils from disadvantaged populations (Finland and Taiwan) reform that promotes independent pupil learning, creativity and critical thinking (Singapore and Taiwan).*
>
> (p. 3)

Ecological systems model

Positive psychology interventions in schools often make a difference for individuals. But what enables all in a school to thrive and learn is a critical ecological approach to wellbeing, and a recognition that this is not an 'add on' but a way of being. An adaptation of Bronfenbrenner's ecological systems theory helps visualise what this means (1979, 2004).

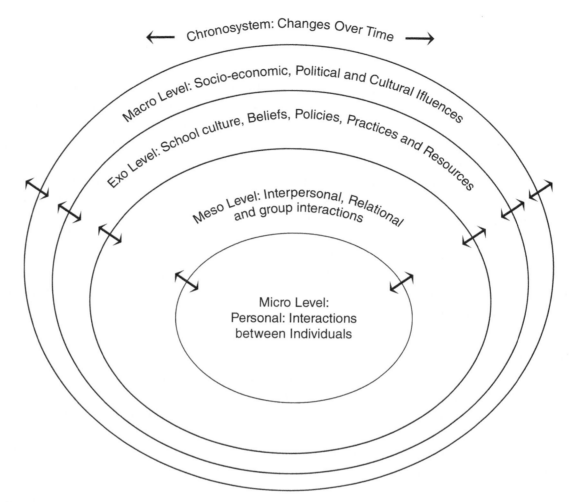

Figure 0.1 Ecological systems model.
(Adapted from Bronfenbrenner.)

The ecological systems model confirms that the most powerful influences on the developing child are in the micro level: these are the interactions that individuals have on a daily basis with those in their immediate vicinity. In schools, this would be with teachers and peers. The words that teachers say to their pupils have a powerful impact on how they perceive themselves and the world of school. The quality of those interactions is embedded in what happens at the meso level, which includes the relationships that these people have with each other. In families, this would be the relationship between parents, with extended family members, neighbours and those in the local community. In schools, it relates to relationships and conversations between teachers, staff and school leadership, what happens in classes, home–school interactions and links with the local community. The exo level for families is how workplaces and communities operate. In schools, this comprises the beliefs, policies and practices embedded in school culture, as well as the resources available. If a school's overriding priority is excellence in learning demonstrated by high grades, then the conversations between teachers will reflect that, and the interactions with pupils will focus primarily on their academic progress. At the macro level are economic-socio-political influences. In the UK this currently determines what is taught, how it is taught, and the ways in which schools are inspected.

These systems, however, are not set in stone. Each level impacts bi-directionally on others. Teachers may feel they are controlled from above, but what they say and do can make a difference, not just for individual pupils but on the systems in which they work. The chrono level in systems theory affirms that changes occur over time. Conversations create culture. They impact on what people believe, on how we position and treat each other, what matters, what we do and what is effective. Teachers change lives in more ways than they know.

What and why ASPIRE?

ASPIRE is an acronym for Agency, Safety, Positivity, Inclusion, Respect and Equity: together these encapsulate the principles underpinning positive education and wellbeing. They apply to everything that happens in a school, family and community. They have been developed over many years and are based in what we know about optimal child development, positive psychology, healthy relationships, a safe, strengths-based pedagogy, how students are motivated and learn and healthy schools. The following is a brief synopsis.

Agency

Agency is power with rather than power over – it is the opposite of control, which is often toxic in a relationship. It incorporates self-determination, intrinsic motivation, self-directed learning, social action and the changing role of teachers in a digital age. Aligned with agency is responsibility, both individual and group. The chapter includes student voice and choice, stakeholder involvement in decision making and whole class responsibility for class culture. Agency is related to citizenship and future community engagement.

Safety

This incorporates physical, emotional, psychological and digital safety. Some students do not feel safe in school. The chapter includes the value of making mistakes, valuing diversity, reducing bullying, promoting collaboration over competition and the value of personal bests so that no pupil considers themselves a loser. This chapter also addresses some major safety issues for young people, such as toxic masculinity and knife crime and how these might be tackled in school.

Positivity

Negative feelings shut down cognitive pathways, so to maximise learning we need to promote the positive wherever possible. This includes using strengths-based language, a solution rather than problem focus, and playfulness – often disregarded in education but valuable for mental health. This chapter outlines the micro-moments of positive action that foster kindness, optimism, gratitude and pro-social behaviour. Solution-focused meetings and teacher wellbeing are also addressed here.

Inclusion

There is now a raft of research on the value of a sense of belonging for resilience and positive adaptation. This includes believing in the best of every pupil, and students not only being valued but being of value. Inclusion in school involves participation, progress with learning and having a recognised role. This chapter outlines the difference between inclusive and exclusive belonging and the importance of giving pupils opportunities to know each other, build connections and foster positive relationships: this goes beyond skill development to our perceptions and understanding of each other. Case studies include the work of Together for Humanity – helping students understand other cultures and value diversity.

Respect

Respect is both for individuals and their ideas, but also for culture, not jumping to judgment without hearing, and understanding diverse stories. This requires good listening. Having cultural and contextual awareness means not imposing the dominant culture but taking account of community and context to promote active inclusion. Respect is demonstrated by adherence to the Golden Rule – treating others as you would have them treat you. We also consider respect for nature and the environment and for human rights.

Equity

Equity is aligned with fairness. There is discussion about 'levelling up', but much less on how education systems might provide opportunities to do this. This requires flexibility, fairness and support. Equity also matters in the staffroom. This chapter looks at all the ways in which students have unique needs and concludes that education needs to be diverse. One size does not fit all. This chapter also explores practices that promote equality and those that are barriers, including access to resources. For a more equitable future, education needs to include active citizenship and critical thinking for all students.

ASPIRE in action across the world

This chapter has case studies from the UK, Australia, China and South Africa putting all the ASPIRE principles into action and the difference this is making.

Although each principle is important in its own right and they are addressed separately in the chapters, they also interact with and reinforce each other. It is the application of all six principles across systems that promotes optimal wellbeing and learning for all.

The structure of the chapters

Each chapter, except for the final one, has a similar structure. The first sections are the theory, rationale and evidence base for the principle, and the rest of the chapter is about putting this into practice with children, teachers and communities:

- What do we mean by the principle? – looking at definitions and applications
- Why does this matter? – including its relevance to wellbeing and learning and congruence with the United Nations Charter of the Rights of the Child
- Putting this principle into practice in the secondary classroom
- Putting this principle into practice in the secondary school
- Social and emotional learning
- A checklist
- Looking ahead – this principle in the future
- References and further reading
- Resources – including websites, podcasts and downloadable materials.

As well as laying out the rationale for ASPIRE, each chapter showcases instances where these principles are happening, and the difference this is making for stakeholders across a school. These case studies and vignettes provide powerful examples of the efficacy of ASPIRE internationally, and have been generously provided by students, teachers, school leaders, psychologists and academics.

Although the text is based in evidence, not everything is cited. This makes it more accessible to the reader. Those who want to know more are directed to the further reading. As the overall focus is primarily on generalities, it is not possible to address everything specifically. My apologies if I have not covered your particular concern.

Social and emotional learning (SEL)

UNESCO's four pillars of learning are: learning to know, learning to do, learning to be and learning to live together (Delors et al., 1996). The first two are the knowledge and skills that have spurred innovation and development across the globe. We have a knowledge base that is truly extraordinary; the internet, space travel, and medical advances are just a few of the many projects that would be in the realm of magic and miracles a century or so ago. But we have not developed wisdom anything like as far or as well. The final two pillars are those needed for, amongst other things, strong, supportive relationships, conflict resolution and mental health, but have rarely had the same priority in educational settings. Learning to be and learning to live together are encompassed in SEL, which needs to be threaded through the curriculum as well as in targeted sessions. These need to happen in a safe, solution-focused space and the outcomes reinforced in everyday interactions. There are activities in every chapter that help students learn together about each principle and ways to action this in their lives.

Secondary settings

The companion book on ASPIRE addresses what needs to happen in early years and primary settings to promote wellbeing and learning for all. The needs of adolescents in secondary schools matter just as much, especially with an increase in those who are clearly not doing so well, especially since the pandemic (Roffey, 2023).

Young people between the ages of 11 and 18 are at a critical age—what happens to them, the opportunities available to them, and the sense they make of the world during these years all have a lasting impact on the rest of their lives. It is the time to explore who they are, who they want to become, and the values they hold.

A risk in secondary education is under-estimating the potential of adolescents. When we have a restricted, inflexible curriculum and a teach-to-the-test learning environment, we are in effect putting metaphorical blinkers and a straight-jacket on a generation of ideas and possibilities. Given a voice and opportunity, young people can often be innovative, active and collaboratively engaged. This is evident in the lead that some have taken on issues such as raising funds for specific charities, education for girls, gun control in the US, and the climate crisis across the world.

A Harvard Survey of 10,000 young people in 33 high schools in the US across a wide spectrum of race, class and culture, however, was published in 2014, and there is little indication that things have changed since. This showed that almost 80% valued personal success and happiness over concern for others. The report goes on to say that when young people do not prioritise caring and fairness over aspects of personal success, they are more likely to engage in behaviour that is cruel, disrespectful and dishonest and take risks with their own wellbeing. Youths were three times more likely to agree than disagree with this statement: *"My parents are prouder if I get good grades in my classes than if I'm a caring community member in class and school"*.

A healthy civil society depends on adults who are committed to their communities and who, at pivotal times, will put the common good before their own. This is most evident when crises strike, such as the volunteer fire-fighters whose primary concern is to save the lives and homes of others, and the doctors, nurses and care-workers who risk their own safety in treating patients with coronavirus and other infectious diseases.

Young people need to not only access knowledge that enables them to navigate the challenges of a fast-changing world, but also learn that authentic happiness, wellbeing and a life well lived, are not about being rich and powerful but about the qualities of our relationships and having a sense of meaning and purpose in life beyond the self. Others matter, and the values of kindness, altruism and respect for diversity build safer and healthier communities. Such positive experiences in education not only construct a world we all want to live in, they also underpin future mental health and wellbeing.

It begins with belief

This book is admittedly idealistic, especially in the current climate. But this can also be seen as its strength. If we do not have a vision for a positive experience in schools for all young people and their future, we risk staying with a reality that is clearly not working for everyone. It should not be possible for anyone to fail in education. We also know, as it is both cited and demonstrated here, that aspiring to ASPIRE is both possible and worthwhile. It begins with belief.

We need an education system fit for purpose for the 21st century, where all pupils thrive and make progress in learning and where wellbeing for everyone is at the heart of a school. Imagine what difference it would make when every young person wants to come to school, feels they matter when they are there, and develops confidence, resilience, curiosity about the world, a positive sense of self and healthy relationships? The evidence-based ASPIRE principles of agency, safety, positivity, inclusion, respect and equity in practice can make that happen. This book shows how.

References, further reading and resources

Bronfenbrenner, U. (1979). *The Ecology of Human Development: Experiments by Nature and Design.* Harvard University Press.

Bronfenbrenner, U. (2004). *Making Human Beings Human: Bioecological Perspectives on Human Development* Sage Publications.

Delors, J. et al. (1996). *Learning: The Treasure Within; Report to UNESCO of the International Commission on Education for the 21st Century.* UNESCO.

Greatbatch, D. & Tate, S. (2019). *School Improvement Systems in High Performing Countries.* Government Social Research, Department for Education.

Harvard Making Caring Common Project (2014). *The Children We Mean to Raise: The Real Messages Adults Are Sending About Values.* Harvard Graduate School of Education.

Noble, T., McGrath, H., Roffey, S. & Rowling, L. (2008). *A Scoping Study on Student Wellbeing.* Department of Education, Employment & Workplace Relations (DEEWR) Australian Federal Government.

Roffey, S. (2023). ASPIRE to a better future: The impact of the pandemic on young people and options for schools post Covid-19. *Education Sciences, 13,* 623.

Street, H. (2018). *Contextual Wellbeing: Creating Positive Schools from the Inside Out.* Wise Solutions.

UNICEF (2007). *A Human Rights-Based Approach to Education for All.* United Nations Children's Fund.

Further reading

Bethune, A. (2018). *Wellbeing in the Primary Classroom: A Practical Guide to Teaching Happiness.* Bloomsbury.

European Commission (2022). *Impacts of Covid on School Education.* European Commission.

Evans, K., Hoyle, T., Roberts, F. & Yusuf, B. (2022). *The Big Book of Whole School Wellbeing.* Corwin.

Giraldez-Hayes, A. & Burke, J. (2023). *Applied Positive School Psychology*. Routledge.

Grenville-Cleave, B., Guðmundsdóttir, D., Huppert, F., King, V., Roffey, D., Roffey, S. & De Vries, M. (2021). *Creating the World We Want to Live In: How Positive Psychology Can Build a Brighter Future*. Routledge.

Kern, M.L. & Wehmeyer, M.L. (2021). *Palgrave Handbook of Positive Education*. Palgrave Macmillan.

Martineau, W. & Bakopoulou, I. (2023). What children need to flourish: Insights from a qualitative study of children's mental health and wellbeing in the pandemic. *Education 3-13, 52*(1), 33–47.

Quinlan, D.M. & Hone, L.C. (2020). *The Educators' Guide to Whole-School Wellbeing: A Practical Guide to Getting Started, Best-Practice Process and Effective Implementation*. Routledge.

Roffey, S. (2012). *Positive Relationships; Evidence Based Practice across the World*. Springer.

Roffey, S. (2020). *Circle Solutions for Student Wellbeing* (3rd Ed.). Sage Publications.

Sharp, C. & Nelson, J. (2021). *Recovering from Covid 19: What Pupils and Schools Need Now*. NFER Policy Briefing.

Sylvester, R. & Seldon, A. (Chairs) (2022). Times Education Commission Report: Bringing out the Best: How to Transform Education and Unleash the Potential of Every Child. *The Times*.

Resources

https://learning.nspcc.org.uk/child-health-development

1 Agency

Power with, not power over

What do we mean by Agency?

If we want young people to become independent, active learners, and participate positively in the world around them, we need to give them opportunities to practice this in education. Agency is the practice of giving people choices where possible, encouraging them to have a voice in what concerns them, but also encouraging them to think through the consequences of different actions, not just for themselves but for others. This enables them to have self-efficacy, a belief they can act – and that what they do has an impact and matters.

Agency and autonomy are often used interchangeably, as both mean being able to make your own decisions and not be controlled by others, but there is a significant difference. Autonomy is striving for your own goals and acting independently, regardless of what is going on around you. We see this in those who chose not to vaccinate against Covid-19 because of their values of personal freedom and not being told what to do. No-one, however, is entirely independent, as actions are influenced by others and the environment. Agency, on the other hand, is making decisions that take account of the context and that are often linked to influencing change and making a difference. We see this in people who did choose to be vaccinated against Covid-19 because this reduced the spread of the disease and protected everyone.

Ryan and Deci's self-determination theory (2000, 2018) has been significant worldwide in challenging the view that people only do things for external reward. The fulfilment of other innate needs matters. The theory comprises three linked components:

- Autonomy is the need for personal freedom to make decisions and be responsible for them.
- Competence is an individual's need to feel that they have mastery over their social environment and outcomes.
- Relatedness is the need to feel a sense of belonging and connection to others.

This mirrors the concept of Agency we refer to here.

There are three dimensions to Agency:

- Having a sense of Agency: the belief that you can make decisions and affect change
- Opportunities to exercise Agency: dependent on context, especially relationships
- The practice of Agency: the capacity and competencies to take action.

Students with a sense of Agency have a belief in their ability to make choices and that these will have consequences. They need to be given opportunities to put Agency into practice and have the skills to do so. If a person is ignored or belittled when they choose to act – whether or not this made a difference – this impacts on their sense of Agency in future similar situations.

DOI: 10.4324/9781003428244-2

If students are faced with a rigid curriculum with no room for creativity, innovation, or the potential to influence change, they may not see themselves as having any ownership of their learning and perhaps not even try to become active, creative learners.

Students will inevitably have a stronger or weaker sense of Agency in different contexts and in relation with varying groups of people, more, for instance, with friends than with teachers.

Agency does not just apply to individuals but also to young people acting together and in families, schools and other organisations. The social, cultural, economic and political context in which these exist determines the extent to which learners are able to make decisions for themselves and how much they are listened to. This will also depend on what is available to them, especially within relationships.

Why does Agency matter?

Congruence with the United Nations Convention on the Rights of the Child

Article 12: Every child has the right to express their views, feelings and wishes in all matters affecting them, and to have their views considered and taken seriously.
Article 13: Every child must be free to express their thoughts and opinions.

These principles recognise children and young people as actors in their own lives and apply at all times throughout a child's life.

Agency is aligned with healthy development, specifically independence and identity, psychological wellbeing, adaptation to adversity, intrinsic motivation, active learning and taking responsibility.

Healthy adolescent development

Adolescence is marked by significant changes in physical development, brain structure, thinking skills, social affiliation, and identity. Getting from childhood to adulthood is not an easy path for many young people, and has been made more difficult by the pandemic: young people need their peers to support them through this process and face-to-face contact has been limited; things have been taken out of their control at a time when they would normally have been becoming more independent, making their own decisions, trying things out and reflecting on options for their future.

Identity

One of the important life skills for adolescents is working out who they are and who they want to be. This incorporates personal and social values, beliefs, sexual identity and goals. There are several stages in this process, and not everyone gets to the final stage of identity achievement:

- Identity 'diffusion' is where there is no firm commitment to a way of being
- 'Foreclosure' is accepting what others say you have to believe, aim for and be. This is likely to happen to young people in closed communities.

Both of these stages are considered less than healthy for the young person's developing sense of self and autonomy.

- Identity 'moratorium' is the process of working this out, exploring alternatives, discussing values with others, and perhaps trying on different personas. This is commonplace with teenagers who may begin by rejecting their family values, potentially causing tension and conflict.
- The final stage is identity achievement, where young people are clear about who they are, what they want out of life, and what is important to them. They may end up with the values they grew up with, but this time they own them for themselves. Some are into adulthood before this happens, and some individuals never get there.

These two stages are considered healthy. Identity achievement offers an established sense of self that fosters resilience, wellbeing and strong relationships (Hansen & Jessop, 2017; Erikson, 1968).

Young people who have experienced trauma in their young lives may continue to be conflicted and confused about who they are and want to be (Berman et al., 2020).

When young people have choices and efficacy, this supports their identity development. When these opportunities are not available, individuals may lack confidence, have low self-worth and not feel able to be proud of who they are becoming. Without the freedom to explore and make choices for themselves, their identity may never fully blossom: they will always be relying on others to tell them what to do and how to be. When these individuals become adult, they may be in positions of authority over others. They are likely to stay with what they have already been told, perhaps because it feels familiar and safe, or even change their position depending on the last person they spoke with. They may maintain the status quo rather than attempt to initiate or change anything. This can lead to organisations becoming 'stuck' rather than innovative.

Wellbeing

Self-determination is now accepted as one of the central pillars of psychological wellbeing (Ryan & Deci, 2018). The satisfaction of the basic psychological needs of autonomy, competence and relatedness promotes healthy functioning at all levels of human development and across different cultures and settings. Martela et al. (2022) found that these needs were aligned with wellbeing across 27 European countries, strongly associated with happiness, life satisfaction, meaning, and lack of depressive symptoms.

When these basic needs are not met, optimal development and positive engagement with the world are frustrated. Students who are routinely controlled by others, either by overprotection or by authoritarian approaches, do not have this basic tenet of wellbeing. Things happen to them rather than with them. It may be hard to stay optimistic, motivated and engaged if you feel that nothing you do makes any difference. It is also harder to develop personal strategies to cope with adversity when you always look to others to resolve issues.

Intrinsic motivation

Motivation is the driver for action. It gives the energy to do things. Many believe that people only do things for external reward – the more you pay someone, the better their performance; the higher your exam results, the more your family and teachers will be pleased. This is extrinsic motivation.

Self-determination theory challenges this view and says that meeting psychological needs is more powerful. People often choose to do things because they are interested in them and enjoy doing them. Sometimes this fits with their values, such as action on climate, or because they want to get better at something – like playing a musical instrument, developing skills in a sport, or learning a language. This is intrinsic motivation.

The drive to explore, experiment and push limits to get better at things is powerful. The political economist Dan Pink (2018) illustrates in his research how often people choose to do things for no external reward, because it has meaning for them in either personal development or community contribution. It gives them eudaemonic happiness – the feeling they are living a good life.

There are many studies which suggest that individuals who are intrinsically motivated are better at learning. In fact, intrinsic motivation is often indicated as one of the most powerful predictors of academic achievement. It is aligned with self-directed learning.

Case study: Jaden

Jaden was not an academic student. He found it hard to sit still and focus in class and did not enjoy books. For the most part, school learning was a miserable experience for him, especially when he went to high school. Most of the time he felt a failure. But he was absolutely brilliant at skateboarding and eventually began to skip school to practice. His teachers and parents despaired, and relationships soured.

Unsurprisingly Jaden didn't get much in the way of exam passes but did begin to develop a skill at helping and teaching younger skateboarders. This was noticed by a local youth group leader, and when Jaden was 17 he was offered the opportunity to volunteer for a few weeks at an orphanage in Thailand. He absolutely loved it and his heart went out to the children in the orphanage. He felt useful. This experience completed changed both Jaden's self-concept and his worldview. He decided that he wanted to make a difference, and when he got home he had the motivation to enrol in a college to get enough qualifications to go to university to study social work. He is now a graduate and enjoying a career that fits him.

Taking responsibility

Once you give someone Agency, they take responsibility for outcomes, whether these are positive or not. If a project is successful, they can rightly feel proud – but if it goes wrong there is no one else to blame. When others are in control it is easy to lay the blame there. Many teachers will have come across pupils who quickly say 'it was them, not me' when something problematic occurs.

The following case study illustrates the immense benefits of enhancing Agency for individuals, their connectedness, future aspirations, and ability to take responsibility, not just for their own actions, but for doing something that makes a difference for others. There are many examples of groups of students taking community action but less often from young people who have begun life with significant disadvantage.

Dubbo Aboriginal Girls Circle

Dubbo College Delroy Campus Aboriginal Girls Circle began in May 2008, and is still going. It is an initiative, originally auspiced by NAPCAN (National Association for the Prevention of Child Abuse and Neglect) to encourage young Aboriginal girls, many of whom come from highly challenging backgrounds, to come together, establish connections both with each other and their culture, inspire change within a diverse community, develop interpersonal skills and build their mental health and resilience.

Girls decide on a major project aimed at building a positive community. They participate in a brainstorm activity in smaller groups and then bring all ideas to the whole group. As a large group, they discuss, debate, investigate options and decide on the final project.

Some of the projects have included:

• Discovering and exploring family trees
• Development of a Friends and Fighting dance – videoed
• Paying It Forward – Random Acts of Kindness initiatives within the school
• Interviews with Indigenous community members about their lives
• Development of Diabetes posters and information sheets to help combat the disease in Indigenous communities.
• The completion of a POSITIVE PATHWAY in the school grounds

The girls create smaller working parties which then reach out to the wider school community to get them involved in the project. The concept of including the whole school was created by the girls to increase morale, increase the sense of belonging, create a safe space for a voice, and enhance their own self-confidence.

As an extra activity, for the last three years, the girls have created Christmas Activity Booklets for the Children's Ward of Dubbo Hospital. The group also then decide who will deliver the booklets, and this has usually been the Year 10 students as representatives of our Girls Circle.

There has been a formal evaluation of the Aboriginal Girls Circle (Dobia et al., 2014), but these quotes show just what it has meant to these Indigenous young women in regional Australia.

What does Girls Circle mean to you?
* *"Being part of a group who want to make a difference in other people's lives."*
* *"The opportunity to do something different from usual schoolwork."*
* *"To meet new people and work as a group on projects to improve young people's lives."*

What have you enjoyed the most?
* *"I have enjoyed doing some fun activities that benefit me as a young person e.g. positive pathway expressing my feelings without being judged."*
* *"I have enjoyed mixing with girls of different ages and learning more about their lives."*
* *"Participating in projects and activities is fun, and seeing how the projects help others is inspirational."*

What difference has it made to your life?
* *"I have learnt that we need to accept people who are different to us."*
* *"I feel like I can express myself better and am not afraid to try new things."*
* *"Learning to listen and show respect to other people has helped me in all of my other classes."*

What difference has it made to your community?
* *"The community has seen what Aboriginal Girls Circle is all about when they looked at our pathway and when we did the Elders' lunches."*
* *"Hopefully people will see that not all young people are causing trouble in the town."*
* *"People ask us to do activities for them, e.g. working with the primary students doing activities."*

How do you think it will make a difference to your future?
* *"I think I will be more confident looking for a job."*
* *"I understand now that it is important to set yourself some goals and do not be afraid to have a go."*
* *"I appreciate that everyone is different but we should all try to work together to make life easier."*

Other quotes:
* *"... made me realise you can do good things without expecting to be paid back."*
* *"... good activities to get to know people."*
* *"... finding other ways to be nice to people and to give back"*
* *"... a chance to connect and help for the better"*
* *"Girls Circle is an opportunity to connect with a range of people and collaborate to create a project."*
* *"A fun group where we can help others and enjoy ourselves."*

Kathryn Bermingham, Deputy Principal, Delroy Campus, Dubbo College, New South Wales

Having been involved with this initiative for many years, I know it would never have got off the ground, let alone achieved sustainable impact, had if it had not been for the commitment and determination of specific staff at the College, especially Kathryn, alongside Aboriginal education officers. Agency needs to be facilitated in schools by those who believe in its value for student lives.

Agency beyond school

You only have to look at initiatives around the world to see that young people are able, willing and enthusiastic about taking action when given the opportunity. This includes the Global Youth Mobilization launched in December 2020 with funding support from the World Health Organization and others. There have been 471 projects in 125 countries, supporting 800,000 communities. These projects have been developed around four main themes:

* Supporting Covid-19 prevention measures and tackling misinformation
* Physical and mental health challenges
* Disruption in education and improving employment prospects
* Overcome gender inequality and combat domestic and gender-based violence.

The report on this initiative is available from the World Health Organization (2023), and voices of some of the young people involved in these projects can be heard in the video in the Resources: "*We are unstoppable together*"

Given the opportunity, young people cannot only influence what is done, but how.

C.A.T.S. – Children as Actors Transforming Society: empathy, evidence and engaged action

From 2013 to 2018, around 300 people each year, over half of them under 18, went up a mountain in Switzerland to stay in a castle for 7 days. It began as an adult-led conference with a basic agenda on peace, democracy and dialogue, and was run by three organisations: Child to Child

Trust, Learning for Wellbeing and Initiatives of Change. Most of the children and young people who attended came through projects supported by international NGOs such as World Vision and Save the Children, from countries as diverse as Ethiopia, Bulgaria, Kenya and Canada.

The first conference was, as you would expect, keynote speakers, break-out discussions and so on. But then things changed. As part of their commitment to Human Rights, Wales had established a Children's Parliament – known as Funky Dragon. These young people were asked to evaluate the conference and were clear that it needed a different model. A working group was set up with young people who identified each year's broad theme – such as inclusion, participation or non-violence – and then set about creating a safe, supported space which was both playful and exploratory to reflect on needs and actions. A popular inclusion was the talking library. This facilitated young people telling their story – about their lives, their struggles, their achievements and their hopes. They wrote a brief synopsis on a 'library ticket', and others would join their table to hear them speak for 15 minutes and then ask more about their story.

These young people turned the conference from a 'top-down' model of information delivery into a forum for the exchange of ideas, the building of friendship, and the development of actions children and young people might take to change their worlds.

Gerison Lansdown, founder director of the Children's Rights Alliance for England and an international children's rights consultant

Agency in education

In some ways the pandemic impacted more on adolescents than on others in the community. Although they were less likely to be seriously ill, the lack of control, reduced independence and social restrictions meant that for some, social and emotional development was interrupted. It is more relevant than ever that schools promote both agency and connection.

According to the OECD (2019), Agency in education is about "*acting rather than being acted upon; shaping rather than being shaped; and making responsible decisions and choices rather than accepting those determined by others*". When young people are routinely told what to do and how to do it, they not only miss out on learning vital life skills, they also are unable to build on their own interests, strengths and concerns.

Teaching and learning

Traditionally education is teacher-directed. When students are positioned as empty vessels to be filled with information that is regurgitated at appropriate moments, the direction of learning is a one-way street. This is not only disrespectful to students and their prior knowledge, but also far from reality. Pupils have information, understanding, ideas and experiences that colour and position new knowledge, so it makes sense for learning to be interactive and build on what students bring.

Agency in education is giving young people more ownership of their learning rather than invariably dictating what they should be doing, how and when. In school, students may learn that what matters are the teachers' choices and judgments. The goal in class, in the minds of many, is not competence and understanding but good grades. A system of constant testing and evaluation in school—which in some countries becomes increasingly intense with every passing year—is a system that substitutes extrinsic rewards and goals for intrinsic ones. It is almost designed to produce anxiety and depression in those whose achievements are not deemed worthy of celebration.

Giving students a sense of Agency needs to be matched by empowering them to take ownership of their learning. When opportunities are provided for pupils to exercise their Agency in relation to various aspects of the learning process, they acquire effective control. Making opportunities explicit and readily accessible enables all students to recognise and tap into their potential.

Agency is not just about pedagogy but also the curriculum. What young people learn about themselves, the world around them and their place in it is configured by curriculum content.

Agency as a principle enhances wellbeing and engagement with education and builds a society where citizens see themselves as potential agents of change.

Agency in practice in the secondary classroom

Research says that secondary students across the world are often bored in school. Most children enter school with enthusiasm for learning, but engagement falls steadily as they go through their education, until nearly half are disengaged by their final year (Ledertoug & Paarup, 2021). Disengagement either means switching off or looking for alternative entertainment, resulting in disruptive behaviour. Although some boredom is due to student disposition, much is down to institutional factors such as curriculum content and teaching method, alongside the quality of the school environment. According to the Times Education Commission Report (Sylvester & Seldon, 2022), the curriculum in English high schools is often seen as irrelevant to the lives and futures of students, and as importantly also to business and employers who are looking for 'creativity and collaborative working'. It is clear that much has to change to make education fit for purpose, not only for the 21st century but for the experiences of young people going through school – and their long-suffering teachers. It makes sense to give students agency over their learning wherever possible.

Self-directed learning

Most adult learning is self-directed. People read books, search for information on the internet, join a class or a group with the aim of achieving something, and practice a skill to get better at it. But how does this translate into teaching approaches so that students become life-long learners? Van Deur and Murray-Harvey (2005) found that successful implementation was dependent on both internal and external factors. These interact with each other with some being dependent on earlier experiences. Although this research was carried out in primary schools, the findings are relevant across settings.

Internal factors:
- The task being presented needs to stimulate interest, creativity and critical thinking.
- Personal characteristics of self-motivated learners include a belief they can do it, willingness to make the effort, and coping strategies to keep going when things are challenging.
- Personal learning strategies include planning, checking and reflecting on what is being achieved.

External factors:
- A school context where student Agency is valued
- Opportunities in the class for enquiry and taking responsibility
- Teacher guidance and coaching, including explicit strategies for self-directed learning
- Classroom organisation, including collaborative learning
- Resources – books, IT, other people.

Examples of teaching approaches that give students Agency

Problem-based learning

Students examine complex, real-world problems, explore and discuss potential solutions, debate the positives and negatives of each idea, and develop a plan to address the problem. This usually happens collaboratively.

Project-based learning

There are many overlaps with problem-based learning, but not every project begins with a problem but with an area for exploration. Teachers may introduce a subject area and give students ideas of how to research this. This can include online research, library research, interviews and drafting questions. Students may work alone or with others and would be expected to deliver their specific findings on a topic to the whole group. Presentations are part of both problem- and project-based learning.

Personalised learning

This is based on the premise that pupils learn at different rates and have different strengths, needs and interests. Personalised learning involves students constructing their own learning pathway, writing their own targets, and then breaking these down into small steps where needed. This aims to engage students in ways that teacher-led approaches cannot (Darling-Hammond, 2017).

Flipped learning

This is where a teacher provides material, digitally or online, that introduces students to a subject. They watch and listen as a homework assignment and then come to class to develop their understanding further by active learning experiences such as discussions, peer teaching, presentations, projects, problem-solving, computations, and group activities. This flips the usual approach of teachers presenting subjects to students who then do assignments at home based on this.

The role of the teacher

There is a pithy saying that the role of the teacher in self-directed learning changes from the 'sage on the stage' to the 'guide on the side'. Teacher knowledge is still needed, but the delivery of this is balanced with other skill sets. Teachers are essential facilitators of self-directed learning in that they:

- introduce the topic in ways that engage interest and attention
- establish a safe learning environment that enables exploration, drafts and learning from mistakes.
- listen to students so they tune into their strengths, interests, difficulties and insights.
- ask searching questions – ensuring that students develop deep and critical thinking.
- are available to answer questions and/or direct students to reliable sources of information.
- set challenges and offer feedback that enables students to develop further understanding and application of knowledge.
- evaluate progress with students and make suggestions for development.
- are a co-learner and co-creator – being engaged in the projects to share learning, success and disappointment.

- celebrate achievements that help students feel pride in what they have done and enhance their motivation.
- construct personal learning checklists with students that affirm what has been achieved and to what level, possibly against criteria.

Teachers used to traditional ways of working, where the same curriculum is delivered to all students, may initially be alarmed at the change of approach needed with more personalised learning. It takes time and training to become effective as a facilitator rather than fount of knowledge. It also requires school leadership, planning and resources. But when students become more fully engaged with learning and appreciate what teachers offer, it can become a much more satisfying profession in which to be working. Where there is national summative evaluation with exams based on memory skills, personalised learning is less likely to take place. Changing the exam system will facilitate learning for all.

There is an assumption that secondary school students are literate. This, of course, is not the case for all. See Chapter 6 on Equity for alternative ways of accessing knowledge and demonstrating understanding.

Teacher–student relationships

There is a spectrum in every school from total adult control to pupils making their own decisions about what works best in their context. This includes what is taught, how it is taught, expectations on teacher time, and what is prioritised in school policies.

Agency in school is facilitated or inhibited by the actions, decisions and beliefs of the adults. This principle is about empowerment – power *with* rather than power *over* – and is the opposite of control, which is invariably toxic in any relationship. Relationships between teachers and students are already unequal, because a teacher has more power than a student. Using this authority to empower pupils is more likely to promote positive behaviour and engagement with learning than asserting power and being authoritarian.

A common discourse on teacher–student relationships is that a 'good' teacher has to be in control of their students, and if they are not chaos will ensue. There are stories in the media about 'out of control' schools, often with a call for 'more discipline'.

A healthy relationship, however, is where there is equality and shared decision-making. A controlling and coercive relationship is now recognised in UK law as toxic and dangerous. Overbearing control in schools does not model positive relationship skills and undermines protective factors in resilience. It is also exhausting and can lead to resentment, reducing rather than increasing the chance of pro-social behaviour. Where pupils are already emotionally volatile it can spark a melt-down. At the far end of controlling relationships, we find bullying and abuse.

In many schools, however, teachers have to deliver a curriculum and get pupils through tests to show what they have learnt. They may feel that the only way to do this is to establish high levels of control. Some students may accept this as they want to please teachers, get good grades, or not get into trouble, but this approach may both undermine a pupil's engagement with a subject and impact negatively on their wellbeing. This is as true for the compliant students as it is for the disruptive ones.

What can teachers do instead when they are pulled in two directions – maintaining/raising educational outcomes and giving students a voice and choice? There is a difference between being in charge of proceedings in a class and controlling students. A teacher who is able to be in charge of proceedings in the classroom, orchestrate events, lead, support, guide, encourage participation, provide timely feedback, and be responsive to individuals as well as the group, does not need to control students. An effective educator encourages self-control and believes in the ability of students to learn this and put responsibility back where it belongs. This aligns with self-directed learning above.

Relationships are enacted by what is said and not said and messages that are given about value and expectations. Words are powerful. They can be used for positive effect but also have the potential for damage.

Glasser (1998) says external control is destructive to relationships and that being disconnected is the source of almost all human problems. He advocates seven caring habits to counter what he calls 'deadly habits' which undermine healthy relationships:

Example of a practical application in school

Deadly habit	Caring habit	Example
Criticising	Supporting	'How can I help you?'
Blaming	Encouraging	'Tomorrow is another day, let's try again then.'
Complaining	Listening	'What happened? What did you want to happen?'
Threatening	Trusting	'I will come back later and see how you have got on.'
Nagging	Accepting	'That didn't go well. How can we move on and make this better?'
Punishing	Respecting	'The decision is yours, but you need to know the consequences.'
Bribing – rewarding to control	Negotiating difference	'Let's see if we can both get what we want here.'

For intrinsic motivation to flourish, pupils must feel free to take risks with their learning and be innovative in responding to challenges, knowing they have the permission, support and respect of their teachers.

Agency in practice across the secondary school

The National Office for Standards in Education (Ofsted) in England recognise the importance of pupil voice in education and have incorporated it into their inspection framework. Schools are expected to provide opportunities for pupils to have their say on matters that affect them and have their views taken into account. Students are encouraged to take on leadership roles and establish student councils as part of this. There is a risk, however, that it will be the more able, confident students who take on these roles, so finding ways to engage diverse voices matters. The following initiative supports agency for all students, including those struggling with their mental health and wellbeing.

Student Voice at St Michael's Church of England High School

Engaging young people in student voice has been fundamental to the success of our school. Providing an authentic and transparent structure between staff and students has helped us develop systems and policies that empower students in shaping their school journey.

Our Student Voice initiative, first launched in 2012 to enhance student and community engagement has evolved organically responding to the changing needs of our school community and gaining significant momentum since the pandemic. Alongside student surveys and focus groups, all students can participate in consultation activities, advisory board meetings, governing body meetings, staff interviews and more.

Our community office is home to Student Voice and has been described by students as 'the place where the magic happens'. Students attend meetings at lunchtime, after school, evenings, and during holiday periods to develop initiatives ranging from fundraising and mental health to work with elderly members of the community. Our inclusive structure offers opportunities to all students, engaging up to 100 members at any given time.

Our journey is evidence that educational establishments who prioritise student voice in its truest form, will reap huge rewards. The universal impact on students is extremely positive, with improved relationships, confidence, resilience, interpersonal skills, leadership and life skills. For others the impact is far greater, offering a sense of belonging when they may have lost their way.

Kerry Whitehouse, School Engagement Development Manager/Senior Mental Health Lead

Dear Student Voice,

When I first came to St Michael's I was hopeful. My last two years of primary school were tough as my anxiety started to get worse and I didn't have the understanding to recognise why I was feeling those emotions so strongly. I was told to toughen up and shut down my feelings, so I wasn't a laughing stock when I arrived at secondary school. I couldn't handle an assembly or a teacher even slightly raising their voice. As year seven went on, things started to get worse, and eventually I realised that I was drowning and needed a lifeboat.

You were that lifeboat. You pulled me out of my ocean of negativity, and while the sun still didn't come out for a period of time after that, you sat with me until it did, teaching me what my anxiety meant, how to help ease it and most importantly that I wasn't alone. I had found my second home and my family, which I owe all to you.

Flash forward to five years later, after what I can only assume have been hours of presenting, days of scripting, weeks of student voice time, months of meetings and years of creating memories. I can proudly say that because of your influence, I am not the same person who walked through the school gates in September of 2017. Of course, I'm not saying that I'm not still in that choppy ocean now, but it's a hell of a lot calmer, and when the storms do roll in, I know how to get out of them on my own. That's because of your advice and your guidance that you've imparted on me over the past five years.

Attending a school that made student agency a key aspect of their ethos solidified the belief that our opinions, thoughts and feedback were highly valued. I think this improved self-confidence within pupils and in turn created an environment where students were at the centre of how the school was run.

I will be forever grateful to have been a part of you.

Jessica Postings, 17, former member of Student Voice

Youth social action

Student willingness and ability to be active and productive members of their communities are often under-estimated. Given opportunities, guidance and support to explore, collaborate and take action, pupils can both contribute to social change and develop positive skills, attitudes and self-concept in the process.

> *Youth social action is happening every day in schools around the country and educators are going the extra mile to provide civic learning opportunities for their pupils.*

(Gunn et al., 2023)

Teachers do not always recognise that raising money for charities, doing sponsored walks or having community events comes under the umbrella of social action, and do not necessarily see this as a valuable tool for learning and wellbeing. They are inhibited from making youth social action a central platform of school culture because of a perceived lack of time and resources to make it happen. But projects do not have to be elaborate or large-scale to be meaningful and can often support the curriculum.

Roger Hart's ladder of participation (1992, 2008) is a way of thinking through the extent to which student participation is authentic. This metaphorical ladder has eight rungs, with each ascending level giving young people increasing decision-making, control, and power. The lowest levels are manipulation, decoration and tokenism, to the highest level, where pupil-initiated decisions are shared with adults.

Service-learning

Service-learning is a teaching and learning strategy that connects academic curriculum to community problem-solving. It is distinct from community service and volunteering, because it focuses on meeting both the needs of the community and that of the learner through a mutually beneficial partnership. Service-learning is integrated with academic curriculum and coursework as *"a form of experiential learning which tests students' higher order thinking skills while deepening their understanding of the subject matter, their community, and themselves."* (youth.gov, n.d.)

Behaviour

There is a concern in the UK and elsewhere that pupil behaviour is worsening – especially since the pandemic. Teachers often struggle with students who have poor concentration, little emotional regulation and are not compliant. Unfortunately, many educators still believe that a behaviourist approach is the way to go. Although it might have immediate impact, it is unlikely to change behaviour beyond the moment, and the same behaviours are likely to re-occur. For our most distressed pupils, whatever sanctions are imposed will not come close to what they are already dealing with. And if we focus on tangible rewards for good behaviour, students may begin to expect such rewards for compliance.

Behaviourist approaches are based on the premise that people only do things out of fear of punishment or for tangible reward. This promotes extrinsic motivation, where pupils learn behaviour 'from the outside in'. Behaviour 'from the inside out' is where learners make their own decisions because it makes them feel good about themselves and promotes a sense of belonging. This will not be effective where students already feel alienated. Feeling good might include getting your own back. Fostering inclusion is linked to pro-social behaviour.

Teachers have to deal with behaviour in the moment it is occurring, but also need to consider what works in the longer term so they don't keep re-inventing the wheel. Positive changes are more likely to occur when strategies and approaches are cohesive and focus on an agentic approach.

It is useful to find out what is going on for pupils and what this means for them and giving them choices about the way forward.

Here are some phrases that might come in useful. Bear in mind that teenagers who are in a high state of emotion will not be able to think straight, so need to have space to calm down first. This also gives teachers a moment they might need to gather their thoughts.

- *"What was going on there? Can you tell me what happened?"*
- *"You were hurting other people – that is not on – but you were clearly angry/upset. Let's talk this through."*

- *"I am at a loss to know how to help here – do you have any ideas?"*
- *"What would help here. Can you draw what you are feeling?"*

Teacher Agency

Many teachers are struggling with educational policies that undermine their voice and choice. It is one reason staff are choosing to leave the profession. It is, however, possible to increase teacher Agency when the senior leadership team maximises consultation. One teacher in a research project told me that she understood that the school executive had to make final decisions but her support for these depended on whether or not she felt genuinely consulted. Having things imposed from above can lead to resentment and subversion. It is not only what happens in schools that matters but how they happen. Using a Circle Solutions format, all staff can engage in discussions about new policies and procedures. This process gives everyone a voice and helps prevent the louder and more confident voices becoming dominant in decision-making.

> **Whole staff consultation**
>
> - The issue is introduced by a member of the senior leadership team, often as a question or challenge to be resolved.
> - Everyone is mixed up so that cliques are disbanded.
> - Staff work in pairs – or a three if there is an uneven number.
> - Partners are given 5–10 minutes to discuss the positives and negatives of the issue, including what is already working well and whether the new initiative aligns with the school's vision.
> - After five minutes they join with another pair to see what they have in common.
> - Each group of four reports what they share and this is written up for everyone to see.
> - This stays up until the next staff meeting to give time for reflection.
> - At the next staff meeting people are again mixed up into groups of four and the staff executive asks for specific input on the issue, based on the earlier discussion. This is where opinions are turned into action and policy. Feedback from each group informs the leadership team, which then makes final decisions taking account of what has been said.
> - Policies are reviewed after a term and tweaked where necessary, using the same format.

Agency in social and emotional learning (SEL)

Agency is demonstrated in SEL when pupils come to their own decisions about values and behaviours rather than being told by those in authority. Activities are presented as games, hypotheticals, discussions and reflections that enable students to think through important issues in their lives in a safe place. Most of the time there are no right or wrong answers, but young people will have had the opportunity to talk with others and reflect on alternative ways of being and living together.

Activities in SEL

Strengths in Circles Cards

There are seven statements for each of the six ASPIRE principles.
   These are four of those for Agency:

* We look for our own solutions.
* We make a difference.
* We can change.
* We give things a go.

In groups of three or four, students take one statement at a time and discuss the following questions together:

– What does this mean?
– Is this what we want in our school?
– What would it make people feel about being here?
– What help do we need?
– Is it already happening – how do we know?
– What else might we do?

Each group decides on one action. They give a brief report back to the Circle, emphasising the action. What they all agree on is put on display as a reminder.

Waste basket and suitcase

(This is based on activities initiated in the Aboriginal Girls Circle to help decide on community action)
   Go around the Circle giving students the name of a sport – football, swimming, skateboarding, running, high jump. You ask people to change places if their sport is called. Pupils then work in random small groups of three or four.
   They are asked to discuss two questions:

1 What in your community do you want to take into your future. What would go in your suitcase? What do you all agree with. Write it down.
2 What in your community needs to change because it will not support a healthy future for everyone. What would go in your waste basket. Write it down.

Give students 8–10 minutes for this activity. Put a waste basket and a suitcase (or shopping bag) in the middle of the Circle. Each group reads out their statements and puts their paper into the appropriate receptacle.
   The teacher collects the statements and looks at what is the most common.

Follow-up activity

Students vote on what they would like to change. In small groups, they explore what they might do – actions that they might take. This could include research on the issue, asking for support, contacting local agencies, or setting up petitions. Future Circles could be devoted to some of this work.

Hypotheticals

Discussions take place in small groups with presentations to the whole Circle.
  First, mix students up so that they work in random groups.

1   *Community action*
    Imagine someone has left some money to your school. About as much as a teacher's
    yearly salary. Each group is a committee responsible for spending this in the best
    possible way. What would make the most difference to the most pupils?

      1st Circle: Each group discusses ideas and decides on the project they want
      to pursue.
      2nd Circle: Planning and making a presentation to the rest of the Circle
      3rd Circle: Each group presents their ideas to the whole Circle to persuade
      others that theirs is the best. There is then a vote.

    Students might like to think about how they might get this action off the ground
    in reality, beginning with checking out what budget they would need and where to
    apply for funds.

2   *Choosing a charity*
    The class is preparing to do some fundraising for a charity. Each group considers
    which area is of most interest to them and they want to work for: The list can
    include but is not limited to the following: health, refugees, children, homeless-
    ness, animals, environment, the aged or human rights. The groups make a case for
    their chosen charity and present to the class who vote for this. This activity can of
    course be taken further as a whole class project deciding on what actions to take to
    raise funds.

Agency checklist

	This is in place – we know it is effective because …	*Working on it – our actions to date are…*	*Just started – our next step will be …*
Pupils spend at least part of the day in self-directed learning and know how to do this			
Pupils are given opportunities to explore and report on interests			
Pupils are encouraged to evaluate their own progress and identify achievements and next steps			
Teachers understand the difference between being in charge of proceedings and controlling students			
Teachers are consulted on policy and practice.			
Social action is part of school culture			

Agency in the future

For a healthy, democratic society, we need active, engaged, responsible citizens who know that they have a voice and can effect change. It is not only knowledge that they need, but confidence and ability to work in teams. Young people collaborating with others to make thoughtful decisions can influence positive change and development from a school to a community to a global level. In order to do this, they must learn to evaluate information, take initiatives, apply their learning, and be able to problem-solve. We under-estimate pupils and their potential if we see them as simply absorbing and then regurgitating information passed on by others, rather than active and interactive in the process of critiquing, understanding and applying knowledge. Unless they have opportunities to have Agency and make a difference when young they may not learn these vital skills, and become dependent on others to create the world they live in.

References, further reading and resources

Berman, S.L., Montgomery, M.J. & Ratner, K. (2020). Trauma and identity: A reciprocal relationship? *Journal of Adolescence, 79*, 275–278.

Darling-Hammond, L. (2017). *What is Personalized Learning and Why Does it Matter?* Learning Policy Institute. learningpolicyinstitute.org/product/personalized-learning

Dobia, B., Bodkin-Andrews, G., Parada, R., O'Rourke, V., Gilbert, S., Daley, A. & Roffey, S. (2014). *Aboriginal Girls Circle: Enhancing Connectedness and Promoting Resilience for Aboriginal Girls: Final Pilot Report.* Western Sydney University.

Erikson, E.H. (1968). *Identity: Youth and Crisis.* Norton.

Glasser, W. (1998). *Choice Theory: A New Psychology of Personal Freedom.* Harper Collins.

Gunn, N., Daly, A. & Tejani, M. (2023). *Make it Authentic: Teachers Experiences of Youth Social Action in Primary Schools.* Royal Society of Arts.

Hansen, D.M. & Jessop, N. (2017). A context for self-determination and agency: Adolescent developmental theories. In M.L. Wehmeyer, K.A. Shogren, T.D. Little & S. Lopez (Eds.), *Development of Self-Determination through the Life-Course* (55–67). Springer.

Hart, R.A. (1992). *Children's Participation: From Tokenism to Citizenship.* United Nations Children's Fund International Child Development Centre.

Hart, R.A. (2008). Stepping back from 'the ladder': Reflections on a model of participatory work with children. In A. Reid, B.B. Jensen, J. Nikel & V. Simovska (Eds.), *Participation and Learning: Perspectives on Education and the Environment, Health and Sustainability* (19–31). Springer.

Ledertoug, M.M. & Paarup, N. (2021). Engaging education: The foundation for wellbeing and academic achievement. In M.L. Kern & M.L. Wehmeyer (Eds.), *The Palgrave Handbook of Positive Education.* Palgrave Macmillan.

Martela, F., Lehmus-Sun, A., Parker, P.D., Pessi, A.B. & Ryan, R.M. (2022). Needs and wellbeing across Europe. Basic psychological needs are closely connected with wellbeing, meaning and symptoms of depression in 27 European countries. *Social Psychological and Personality Science, 14*(5), 1–14.

OECD. (2019). *Future of Education and Skills 2030 A Conceptual Framework Student Agency for 2030.* oecd.org/education/2030-project/teaching-and-learning/learning/student-agency/Student_Agency_for_2030_concept_note.pdf

Pink, D.H. (2018). *Drive: The Surprising Truth about What Motivates Us.* Cannongate.

Ryan, R.M. & Deci, E.L. (2000). Self-determination theory and the facilitation of intrinsic motivation, social development, and well-being. *American Psychologist, 55*(1), 68–78.

Ryan, R.M. & Deci, E.L. (2018). *Self-Determination Theory: Basic Psychological Needs in Motivation, Development and Wellness.* Guilford Press. [An introductory sample chapter is available online: guilford.com/excerpts/ryan.pdf?t=1]

Sylvester, R. & Seldon, A. (Chairs) (2022). *Times Education Commission Report: Bringing Out the Best*. The Times.
Van Deur, P.A. & Murray-Harvey, R. (2005). The inquiry nature of primary schools and students' self-directed learning knowledge. *International Education Journal*, 5(5), 166–177.
World Health Organization. (2023). *Global Youth Mobilization Report*. globalyouthmobilization.org/impact/
youth.gov (n.d.). *Service-Learning*. youth.gov/youth-topics/civic-engagement-and-volunteering/service-learning

Other sources and further reading

Arthur, J., Harrison, T., Taylor-Collins, E. & Moller, F. (2017). *A Habit of Service: The Factors that Sustain Service in Young People*. University of Birmingham: The Jubilee Centre for Character & Values.
Bandura, A. (2008). An agentic perspective on positive psychology. In S.J. Lopez (Ed.), *Positive psychology: Exploring the Best in People Vol 1 Human Strengths*, (167–196). Praeger.
Pink, D.H. (2010). *RSA Animate: Dan Pink – the surprising truth about what motivates us*. youtube.com/watch?v=u6XAPnuFjJc
Roffey, S. (2019). *The Secondary Behaviour Cookbook*. Routledge.
Sirkko, R., Kyrönlampi, T. & Puroila, A.M. (2019). Children's agency: opportunities and constraints. *IJEC*, 51, 283–300.
Sorbring, E. & Kuczynski, L. (2018). Children's agency in the family, in school and in society: implications for health and well-being. *International Journal of Qualitative Studies on Health and Well-Being*, 13(sup1). [This is the introduction to a special edition of the journal. All papers are open access.]
Twenge, J.M., Zhang, L. & Im, C. (2004). It's beyond my control: A cross-temporal meta-analysis of increasing externality in locus of control, 1960–2002. *Personality and Social Psychology Review*, 8, 308–319.
Wehmeyer, M.L., Hyeson Cheon, S., Lee, Y. & Silver, M. (2021). Self-determination in positive education. In M.L. Kern & M.L. Wehmeyer (Eds.), *The Palgrave Book of Positive Education*. Palgrave Macmillan.

Resources

Agency in Action; Chartered College: my.chartered.college/impact_article/pupil-agency-in-action-developing-curriculum-and-pedagogy
OECD Student Agency for 2030: oecd.org/education/2030-project/teaching-and-learning/learning/student-Agency
Roger Hart's Ladder of Participation: organizingengagement.org/models/ladder-of-childrens-participation
www.superkind.org A free platform for schools to bring social action and philanthropy into the classroom.
The Role of Agency in Learning; https://theeducationhub.org.nz/agency
Pupil Voice and Ofsted home.smartschoolcouncils.org.uk/bloglist/2023/3/20/pupil-voice-and-ofsted
World Health Organization. Global Youth Mobilization (2023). Video – We are unstoppable together https://globalyouthmobilization.org

2 Safety

Physical, emotional, social, psychological and digital

What do we mean by Safety?

There are grim stories about how some schools operated in the past – and not just in fiction. They were places of cruelty where pupils were brutalised by staff and expected to bully and intimidate each other. Punishments were harsh and meted out for a wide variety of misdemeanours. Children and young people who 'couldn't take it' and showed distress were ridiculed. Pupils learned to shut down feelings for themselves and for others. Empathy and kindness were considered 'soft', and it was not so much the survival of the fittest but the survival of the meanest – especially for boys. This was not just in schools for local children but also in more privileged echelons of society, where families sent their children away as young as seven to get a 'good education'. We see the impact of such regimes in the attitudes and behaviour of some people today who believe that 'strong discipline' is the way to get students to 'behave' and that positive relationships are not a feature of an effective classroom. They are not interested in the evidence that says otherwise, because their educational experience 'didn't hurt me' – except that it did, in ways they may not fathom. They may have learnt ancient history, classics and calculus but they didn't learn about love, positive connection, healthy relationships and authentic wellbeing. Unless, of course, they had exceptional teachers looking out for them and providing role models.

Although all schools now have safeguarding procedures in place, Safety across the learning environment is much more than policy documents. It is included here as a positive education principle because students need to feel safe at school in order to thrive and learn. Evidence suggests that pupils may have a less positive view of Safety in their school than staff do – so it is worth checking in with them.

Safety is physical, social, psychological, digital and emotional, and there are overlaps between these. Physical Safety means a learning environment where pupils are not at risk of physical harm. Social Safety means acceptance and support from peers, while psychological Safety is freedom from fear of violence, harassment, bullying and intimidation, both actual and witnessed. Digital Safety includes not being exposed to dangerously misleading, coercive or threatening material online, and knowing how to keep yourself and others free from harm. Emotional Safety is being able to maintain a positive sense of self by not being seen as a 'loser', humiliated, rejected or negatively labelled but by having people around who tune into your strengths and acknowledge and encourage your progress.

Safety in school is where pupils are accepted for themselves and free to learn, communicate, ask questions and seek help without fear of ridicule or punishment. They do not need to be hypervigilant in case someone attacks them, either physically or verbally. Feelings of Safety are not generally enhanced by barbed wire, armed guards or a set of rules beginning 'don't', but by a sense of positive community where everyone matters and feels supported and cared for. It is where there is a culture of respect and high expectations for how we treat each other.

DOI: 10.4324/9781003428244-3

The impact of the pandemic

Although lockdowns were put in place to protect people from illness, safety has been compromised in many ways since the pandemic, especially for children and young people. Alongside a higher incidence of hospitalisation for child cruelty and reports of family violence, social media use increased by about 10%. Although this is often considered a safe space for social interaction and entertainment as well as learning, it also presents risks to both safety and healthy development. During lockdown gambling became more prevalent, reaching younger groups, especially boys. Social media also exposes users to images that present idealised looks, unattainable except by a very few – adding to the perception of not being 'good enough'. The United Nations Office on Drugs and Crime estimates that globally 60% of all enrolled learners were affected by school closures. Adolescents were therefore at a higher risk of exploitation, violence, and abuse, including recruitment by terrorist and other criminal networks.

If students are in school or otherwise engaged in supervised activity, they are safer. Making education relevant, engaging, and enjoyable, as well taking place in a safe environment is necessary to encourage young people back into learning.

Why does Safety matter?

Congruence with the United Nations Convention on the Rights of the Child

Article 3: The best interests of the child must be a priority in all decisions and actions that affect children.
Article 19: Protection from violence, abuse and neglect. Governments must do all they can to ensure that children are protected from all forms of violence, abuse, neglect and bad treatment by their parents or anyone else who looks after them.

Students who feel safe at school are more likely to be able to concentrate and learn. Positive emotions foster creativity and problem-solving, whereas anxiety shuts down cognitive pathways and impedes attention.

Students need to be able to trust that the adults around them have their best interests at heart. If a pupil is worried about what will happen if they make mistakes, they may resist trying or taking risks with their learning. This limits their knowledge and understanding and undermines attainment. When educators are so focused on results that they do not have the time or resources to find out what would help those who are struggling, young people may not feel safe in school. Insecurity may make them more likely to stay with what is familiar and comfortable rather than seeking challenges and mastery.

Insecurity also inhibits social relationships when pupils can be wary or even scared of others. Especially during the pandemic, there were significant numbers of young people who experienced loneliness, and many continue to feel isolated. This constitutes a serious risk to their mental health and wellbeing.

Bullying in school can have far-reaching consequences for both the bully and the bullied. When individuals are routinely put down, ridiculed, intimidated, ganged up on, pushed around, excluded and disempowered, they feel useless, helpless, scared and generally unsafe. They may develop both physical and psychological problems that can last into adulthood. It is one of the main reasons that pupils opt out of school. Those who bully may be at risk of further anti-social behaviour, addictions and family violence, although this also aligns with the experiences that may have led them to bully in the first place, such as aggressive role models and/or lack of emotional support. Witnessing bullying behaviour at school can also lead to anxiety, depression and poor attendance.

Unwanted sexual attention also makes pupils and sometimes staff feel unsafe, especially girls and women. This includes sexual remarks, offensive gestures, sexualised images or graffiti, exposure of genitals, touching that is either overt or falsely 'accidental', to serious sexual abuse, forcing someone to have physical contact against their will. This may be perpetrated by an individual or by a group and is more likely in an environment where toxic masculinity has been allowed to thrive.

For some pupils the fear of going to school may be overwhelming. This can result in doing everything they can to stay home. Persistent absence from school may lead to increased vulnerability, disadvantage and negative life trajectories. Outcomes, however, depend on the personal characteristics of the pupils, the reasons for their absence and the support from home. Punitive measures are counterproductive. See Chapter 4 on Inclusion for more on this.

UK Safeguarding Procedures

In the UK there are published guidelines about what schools should do to protect students from maltreatment, prevent the impairment of their physical or mental health and development, ensure that young people have safe and effective care, and take action to ensure that they have the best outcomes. There is an emphasis on early identification of potential abuse or neglect, whether that is for young or older students, and the document includes a list of issues that are likely to make pupils more at risk, such as being a young carer; being disabled; having an education, health and care plan; being persistently absent from school; or living with family members who are coping with addiction, imprisonment or violence.

> *Safeguarding and promoting the welfare of children is everyone's responsibility. Everyone who comes into contact with children and their families has a role to play. In order to fulfil this responsibility effectively, all practitioners should make sure their approach is child centred. This means that they should consider, at all times, what is in the best interests of the child.*
>
> (DfE, 2022)

Schools have to appoint a designated safe-guarding lead, responsible for ensuring that teachers are aware of potential issues for pupils, responding to concerns that are raised, and liaising with others in the community, such as social services.

Although much in the guidance is positive and supportive and is a concerted attempt to stop children and young people falling between the cracks, concern has been expressed over the extent of paperwork involved. There is a view that safeguarding in some schools has become a tick-box activity that meets inspection requirements, rather than an authentic learner-centred response to need and the establishment of a safe, warm and respectful school environment. There is also a lack of confidence that the requirement to report suspected abuse will be followed up promptly, as there are not enough personnel in social service departments to do this. Concerns about pupil Safety have risen since the pandemic with many students not returning to school.

Australian Safe Schools Framework

In Australia the focus on Safety is more pro-active, and strongly aligned with wellbeing for all.

> *All Australian schools are safe, supportive and respectful teaching and learning communities that promote student wellbeing.*

The Framework identifies nine key elements to assist schools in planning, implementing and maintaining a safe, supportive and protective learning community that promotes student Safety and wellbeing:

1   Leadership commitment to a safe school
2   A supportive and connected school culture
3   Policies and procedures
4   Professional learning
5   Positive behaviour management
6   Engagement, skill development and safe school curriculum
7   A focus on student wellbeing and student ownership
8   Early intervention and targeted support
9   Partnerships with families and community.

These are the components of element 6:

6.1   A strong focus on the enhancement of student engagement with learning
6.2   The extensive use of cooperative learning and other relational teaching strategies
6.3   Teaching of skills and understandings to promote cyber Safety and for countering harassment, aggression, violence and bullying
6.4   Teaching of skills and understandings related to personal safety and protective behaviours
6.5   Teaching of social and emotional skills (e.g. listening, negotiation, sharing, empathic responding) in all subjects and across all year levels.

Details of all other elements can be found on the website listed in the References at the end of this chapter.

Safety in practice in the secondary classroom

Physical Safety in school is critical to protect pupils who are more vulnerable. This could include those born with specific difficulties who need a supported environment, those who have temporary needs such as broken bones, and those who have chronic illnesses including diabetes, coeliac, asthma and allergies. This last is now a serious issue in schools, with a substantial rise in dangerous reactions to specific foods, insect stings, and substances such as aspirin and latex. An anaphylactic attack caused by ingesting an allergen either through the mouth or skin can be fatal without rapid action. All adults in a school need to know what to do.

Good practice saves lives

In Australia every staffroom has photographs of students with allergies, with information about the different substances they are allergic to. Every teacher knows who is at risk and from what. They know what the symptoms of an anaphylactic attack are so can take immediate action. There are adrenaline auto-injectors (epi-pens) in every classroom, and teachers have been trained how to use them in the event of an emergency. This can save lives and needs to be replicated in every school everywhere.

Following some high-profile cases of young people suffering a cardiac arrest in school, there is now a proposal in the UK to have defibrillators in all state schools alongside training in how to use these.

Teacher–pupil relationships: building trust and Safety

Consistency and reliability

When adults are reliable and consistent they build and maintain trust. This includes being careful of what they say and only promising what can be delivered. Routine is also important, so pupils can predict what is going to happen and develop competence in understanding expectations. When changes in routine are signalled clearly and in good time students have more chance to adapt, finalise what they are doing, and not be alarmed by the unexpected. Even minor transitions can be particularly challenging for those who are neurodiverse, so giving a clear warning of change can limit anxiety reactions.

Kindness

This is encapsulated in what is said to pupils. When conversations are warm, strengths-based and encouraging, young people may lose the fear of being ridiculed or demeaned. This is especially important for those whose behaviour reflects unsafe experiences elsewhere.

Being listened to

All young people need to know that they will be taken seriously and that their concerns will not be minimalised or dismissed. When they feel secure in the people around them they are able to ask for help when they need it. It is not always easy for busy teachers to attend to one individual when there are many other things going on in the class, but when pupils know when an adult in school will be available that gives them access to a valuable resource. Although pupils need to be assured that what they say will not be shared widely, they cannot be told that it will be kept confidential if they or someone else is at risk of being hurt.

Teaching and learning

A safe learning environment enables students to take risks and try things out, ask questions, and seek help when needed. Safety in learning is complex and aligned with a sense of self. Many pupils have such a focus on perfection that they never feel good enough. Others don't make an effort, because they see themselves as failures – and never feel good enough! Schools can raise motivation and Safety in learning by changing language, reducing individual comparisons, promoting collaboration over competition, and welcoming mistakes as part of learning.

Language

Comment on what has been achieved, however small. Then ask what the student will do next. Praise effort rather than ability. Self-evaluation is also useful, as this promotes intrinsic motivation and encourages students to take on learning challenges.

Personal bests

Pupils understand this concept from sport. Once someone is competing against themselves they are never a loser – and more likely to value their own progress.

Cooperative learning and project-based approaches

When students are working together they will learn from each other in both research and discussion. One of their tasks could be to devise questions to ask about a topic.

See Chapter 1 on Agency for more on this.

Safety in numbers

Some students are embarrassed by being put on the spot in a class, even if they know the answer. When a question is opened up to all, it is the dominant and confident pupils who quickly put their hands up. Using the Circle Solutions strategy of asking students to discuss an answer in pairs not only relieves anxiety for some but also gives more pupils opportunities to have a voice.

Mistakes

When these are acknowledged as a stage in learning, pupils will be less reluctant to have a go. Using scaffolding and steps towards completion of a task also helps. All writers know the value of drafts and critique: students can also understand this concept and need opportunities to develop these skills.

Practice

Not many of us can master a skill first time around. Opportunities to practice are valuable – especially when they can be positioned as games. This might be the role of homework.

Celebration

Many schools only celebrate sporting and academic achievement, but learning is about all the UNESCO four pillars: learning to know, learning to do, learning to be, and learning to live together. Celebrating all of these gives them credibility and gives more students a chance to shine.

Safety in practice across the secondary school

Knives in schools

The level of knife crime amongst youth has been of growing concern in many countries, and one of the biggest threats to Safety in school has been the increase in young people bringing knives onto the premises. Although actual violence is perpetrated by comparatively few individuals, the impact has much wider implications. It undermines feelings of safety for everyone else, and fear can invade a whole neighbourhood, including local schools. In certain areas, teenagers carrying a knife has become 'normal', something everyone does, often without thinking.

In New South Wales, Australia, there are severe penalties for bringing a knife into school (or anything else that could be used as a weapon) with fines ranging from $4,000 to $11,000 and up to 4 years in jail. The knife does not have to be on the person – perhaps in their locker – but the law still applies. Any knives required for lessons are provided by staff. Similar laws apply to having weapons in a public place, and it is illegal to sell a knife to anyone under 16.

Carrying a knife is against the law in Britain too, but that does not seem to be working in preventing the growing numbers of young people who take knives to school, often claiming that this is 'for their safety'. Injuries with sharp objects are rising twice as fast with 10- to 19-year-olds than in any other age group. If a young person carries a knife, they are likely to use it in situations where they feel the need to protect themselves, commit a crime, intimidate others, or reinforce their status/reputation.

Some schools have instituted random stop-and-search sessions with metal detectors, which they say makes students think twice about bringing weapons to school. In high-crime areas some have also employed security guards, but this reduces their budget for other resources.

Where punitive measures do not effectively address the problem, educational interventions may have more success. This includes some or all of the following – raising awareness of:

- Alternative strategies to managing conflict – using videos, personal stories and role-play activities to emphasise that there is always a choice
- The risks and consequences of carrying a knife
- The impact of knife crime on learning, mental health and future opportunities
- The grief of losing people and the wider impact on families

And

- Myth-busting – such as the notion that carrying a knife makes you safer
- Self-defence classes to give students options to protect themselves without weapons
- First-aid classes so that young people know what to do if a friend has been stabbed
- Building trust between young people and authorities, including providing positive role models that pupils can relate to
- Encouraging reporting of knife crime and making it possible to do this anonymously.

There are websites and other resources at the end of this chapter.

There is a link between knife crime, gangs, and young men growing up believing they have to be 'hard' to be respected and accepted.

Toxic masculinity and Safety: Growing good men

There have been multiple stories in the media about misogyny in various public services, and the danger to women and girls that emanates from this. Much of the focus has been on improving the vetting of new recruits, but every one of the men who hold these views has been a boy who went to school. If we want a society free of toxic masculinity, then what happens in the learning environment matters. This is not only important for both the current and future Safety of women and girls but also for the wellbeing of boys and men, their own mental health and the health of their relationships. Relationships are at the heart of our wellbeing and a life well lived.

It is in their teenage years that adolescents work out who they want to be. Social media influences teenage boys when they are told that girls and women are stopping them from being 'real men' who have a right to be 'respected', and that they are entitled to be in control and powerful. For some adolescents this can be appealing. Where boys have not had positive role models, either because of absent fathers or witnessing family violence, and gender education has been absent in school so far, they may choose this negative stereotype.

When the culture around them also promotes tough-man images, and conversations amongst their peers or influential adults regularly denigrate and dehumanise women, then misogyny is more likely to become entrenched. Although things overall are changing for the better, with more men being closely involved with their families, willing to show emotion, and seeing the advantages of gender equality, there is still a significant proportion who believe not only in traditional masculinity but that the male gender is superior and that women should be submissive and stay 'in their place'. In some environments this belief becomes dominant, and young men either actively enact this or passively do not challenge it. Speaking out may be unsafe unless there are structured opportunities to discuss issues that build a culture of consent, safety and equity.

We need to think about how we can support boys to grow into 'good men' who are proud of their gender, able to establish and maintain healthy relationships, are tuned into their own emotions, can regulate and express these safely, connect meaningfully with others, and in doing so protect their own mental health and the safety of women and girls.

Schools can take actions that increase gendered Safety for everyone:

- Positive role models can be powerful, not only respected male teachers but also men who have qualities that boys often admire, such as sporting prowess, but who also demonstrate qualities of character and are outspoken about respect for women
- Staff who use language that disrespects women are quickly challenged by both colleagues and the school leadership
- Activities are not stereotyped by gender, so that both girls and boys are routinely offered the same opportunities to develop interests and skills
- Images presenting both men and women in non-stereotyped professions and roles are displayed around the school
- Ensuring that groupings in class are mixed-gender
- Challenging statements that exonerate unhelpful gendered stereotypes – e.g. "*Boys will be boys*" or "*you're behaving like a girl*" – or promote the suppression of emotions – such as "*man up*"
- Helping all students to understand the biology of emotion and discuss the skills of emotional regulation and the importance of attaining this
- Stories that challenge the typical 'male hero' strong man and offer alternatives for how to be
- Providing regular opportunities in social and emotional learning (SEL) for structured conversations about what a positive relationship looks and sounds like, the value of healthy relationships for wellbeing, and the attitudes and skills involved
- Providing opportunities for gender-mixed pairs of students to find commonalities to break down prejudice and stereotypes
- Male-led sessions that make issues of male identity overt and discuss choices of being 'a real man' or a 'good man' (See SEL activities at the end of this chapter).

NB: Safety for those who are sexually diverse is covered in Chapter 4 on Inclusion, as is the issue of gang membership.

Safety and consent

Consent can be simply defined as willing agreement by all parties to be involved in a specific behaviour. It is worth adding 'informed' consent so that everyone understands exactly what they are agreeing to and the risks they might be taking. Consent cannot be given if someone is threatened or intimidated, or they are under the influence of drugs or alcohol, or they do not have the capacity to understand. This is not just about consent to a sexual encounter but also to other actions that need to be free choice. If someone changes their mind about something they are effectively withdrawing consent, and their right to do so should be respected. Activities such as sharing photos online without the consent and express permission of that person are not only illegal but an infringement of the human right to privacy and ethically unacceptable.

Consent education is now mandated in all Australian schools from foundation to year 10. In the UK it is included in relationship and sex education, which was mandated in 2020 with the proviso that parents can withdraw their children from sex education.

Consent, however, cannot be a one-off lesson to have impact. Although we can teach pupils what the law says, discussions need to go into greater depth to incorporate values, rights, peer pressure, empathy and diverse experiences. They can include how to ask for consent, checking whether someone is comfortable with what is happening, and being prepared to change direction if a person appears increasingly unhappy. Alongside other aspects of healthy relationships, consent is a whole-school issue. Building a culture of consent can include asking for something rather than just taking, calling out misogynistic or homophobic language and exploring what respecting boundaries means in any interaction.

Digital Safety

Being online is now an integral part of nearly all our lives, with young people routinely using a variety of devices to access social media, games, websites, communications and search engines. Internet use increased during the pandemic, with online Safety becoming an ever-increasing concern. Students need to be aware of the dangers and know how to protect themselves, especially as they are often now expected to use online resources within education. Digital safety is compromised by the following:

- Sharing personal information that may be used to access accounts or steal identities
- Undermining security by sharing passwords – this can lead to being hacked
- Sharing confidences that compromise the safety and wellbeing of others
- Linking with people you don't know. Never agree to meet in person those you have only met online – they may be lying about their age – and everything else
- Collaborating with cyber-bullying by passing on rumours or sharing images
- Posting images that you may regret later
- Reposting messages that are racist, sexist, misogynistic or homophobic
- Watching content that includes extreme violence, sexually explicit or misogynistic images, hateful or offensive material, or false or misleading information.

Conversations about digital Safety in school need to focus on being part of the solution rather than part of the problem:

- Trust your gut – if something doesn't feel right, tune into this, check it out, and do something to stop it
- Be aware of what you post online and consider not just the impact now but in the future
- Call out others who are compromising safety online
- Check in with those who are being hurt to show they have support
- Websites have a responsibility to protect users – report cyber-bullying and hate posts.

Digital safety is never compromised by kindness.

Behaviour

When students have experienced conflict, rejection or trauma, they are often alert to potential negativity in their environment – their default position is not to feel safe. This means that their amygdala – the organ in the brain that reacts to perceived threat – will be triggered by anything that bears any, even faint, resemblance to earlier events. When the amygdala goes into action it prepares the body to fight, freeze or flee. Instructions from the brain to do this are rapid – much faster than the neo-cortex, the thinking part of the brain. This means that reasoning with anyone in an 'amygdala moment' is not viable. This is what needs to happen instead:

Managing amygdala moments

- Minimise perceived threat by standing back and not invading personal space. This also means not thrusting fingers or face towards the person and keeping hands down.
- Keep voice low and slow.
- Acknowledge and validate the emotion being expressed – this shows the student that their distress has been 'heard' and may reduce the need to express it more forcefully.
- Where possible give an instruction or suggestion to do something, not stop something – it's easier to comply.
- Keep others away from potential fallout.
- When possible, suggest that the student move to a quiet space.
- Show care and comfort and do not ask 'why'.
- Once there is calm, it may be helpful to ask "what happened to make you so upset?" Do not press for an answer if that is not easily forthcoming. It is possible that the student won't know, especially if it was a sensory trigger to a traumatic memory.

Safety from bullying

A major threat to Safety in school is bullying. Bullying is not a one-off incident of aggression but repeated acts of verbal and physical intimidation, manipulation, humiliation, exclusion and other micro-cruelties that are perpetrated by one or more pupils who see themselves as wielding power over a less confident peer, often someone who is different in some way from others, perhaps with a disability or specific ethnicity or is considered to be gay. It is invariably supported, either overtly or covertly, by others, who may be fearful that they will be the next target or want to feel powerful themselves. The outcome for young people who are bullied can be severe and can include depression, anxiety, sleeping and eating difficulties, low self-esteem, poor self-worth, helplessness, refusal to come to school and loneliness. Cyber-bullying can mean that there is no escape, even when at home. Bullying also negatively affects those who witness this behaviour because it reduces their own feelings of Safety in school.

Anti-bullying policies are often reactive to perpetrators, usually imposing sanctions. It may be that young people bully others because this is happening to them, so punishment may not change this behaviour over the longer term. If they are being hurt at home, involving parents may exacerbate this. Responses need to be sensitive with consideration for the potential consequences. Sometimes the focus is on the pupils who are bullied, showing them ways to cope and what to do if they find themselves being intimidated, such as walk away. This is useful, but it takes courage and might be risky. We have to think differently.

Bullying can only really thrive in a culture that turns a blind eye. More than anything students need support from others in a school that generates empathy, together with practices that make it more difficult for bullying behaviour to be swept under the carpet. A bystander is someone who sees bullying behaviour taking place but does nothing about it. Upstanders take action. See the SEL section at the end of this chapter.

Teacher Safety

Most educators want positive interactions with families and do their best to foster these. There are times, however, when teacher Safety is at stake when adults arrive in school in a rage. There are ways to handle this that de-escalate confrontation, maximise Safety, and do not damage future relationships.

Safe meetings with families/carers

If the individual is drunk or under the influence of drugs, call for the assistance of another member of staff and suggest that the person leave. You may like to say that you will make an appointment to see them when you can have a constructive conversation. Ask when a good time for them would be to meet with you. Perhaps suggest that they bring a partner or friend to support them. It is also possible that the person is having a breakdown. The same applies, as you cannot resolve any concern in such circumstances.

If the family member is sober but angry, invite them into a classroom or office and ask them to sit down: it is harder to maintain fury when seated. Take a chair yourself near an open door and then use active listening skills until their rage has run its course. Going on the defensive is never useful, so, wherever you can, validate their concerns. When they run out of steam, say something positive about their child and that you are pleased they have taken the trouble to come and talk with you. This may help them appreciate that you both want the best for this pupil and you would like to sort out their issue. Reassure them that they know their child best – this positions them as the expert and will reduce the power imbalance that may be at the heart of their aggression.

Some parents may feel that unless they shout and scream at someone in authority they are not heard and nothing gets resolved. This may be how they have experienced issues in the past. Use a solution-focused framework that explores what a resolution would look like for them and then give the pros and cons of various options, including whether their ideas are feasible and in line with school policies. Decide on a plan where possible and agree on a review date, so that the parent knows you are on their side.

Teacher Safety in the staffroom is similar to pupil Safety in the classroom. I once worked with senior academics who were intimidated in faculty meetings. The leadership team dominated all decisions. Unless you were part of a favoured team of acolytes, your opinion was unwanted, and any contribution to discussion consequently belittled. This toxic environment undermined trust, coloured conversations and good people left. Safety needs to be threaded through the entire school system to enable everyone to give of their best.

Safety in social and emotional learning (SEL)

Safety can be compromised in SEL if pupils are invited to talk about personal issues and feelings in a public forum. This can risk discomfort, embarrassment, or anxiety for students and is a worry for teachers who may not have the time, resources or training to respond effectively with sensitivity during the session– although all disclosures of harm need to be followed up as soon as possible. It is crucial that students have opportunities to discuss, reflect on and make decisions about ways of being, but they need to do this in a secure environment.

Safety in Circle Solutions is maintained in several ways:

- Almost all activities take place in pairs, small groups and the whole Circle. There is no individual competition.
- There is the right to 'pass'. No-one has to speak if they choose not to. Respecting this decision means not going back to anyone individually by name to encourage a contribution. The teacher may, however, ask the whole Circle if anyone has now thought of something they wish to say.
- The focus is on issues, never incidents. Pupils are regularly provided with opportunities to discuss hypothetical situations. This enables issues to be addressed in impersonal ways that do not risk breaching confidentiality.
- There is no naming or blaming.
- The use of the third person rather than first, such as replacing "I" and "me" and "my" with "someone" or an abstract term. Instead of "*It makes me happy when…*" a safer sentence completion is "*It would make someone happy if…*" or "*Happiness is…*". Although students are likely to say things that refer to themselves, they are not expected to.

Activities in SEL

Strengths in Circles Cards

There are seven statements for each of the six ASPIRE principles.
  These are three of those for Safety:

* We are reliable and honest.
* We look out for each other.
* We can get help.

In groups of three or four, all students take one of these statements and discuss the following questions together:

– What does this mean?
– Is this what we want in our lives
– What would it make people feel about being here in school?
– Is it already happening – how do we know?
– What else might we do?

Each group decides on one action. They give a brief report back to the Circle, emphasising the action. What they all agree on is put on display as a reminder.

Stay Away

This activity introduces things to do and say when someone makes unwanted sexual advances. It encourages appropriate assertiveness.

Part One:

Mix students up so that they work in random pairs. They go through the following list together and discuss what is a better option and why. The answers are in Part Two below, with reasons.

Someone approaches you and makes suggestive comments about wanting to have a sexual encounter with you. Think about the options available and discuss what you would do and why.

Actions and Words		**What is better and why**
1	If someone is coming too close to you, move away or	say to them something like 'I need more space' or 'I need you to step back'.	
2	Ignore a sexual comment or	make it clear you are not interested.	
3	Smile or	keep a blank face.	
4	Look directly at the person or	avoid eye contact.	
5	Speak quietly or	as loud as you can.	
6	Say 'Just go away' or	'I want you to leave me alone'	
7	Always tell the truth or	lie if it helps (e.g. 'I have a boyfriend').	
8	Stay silent and move away	try to persuade them to leave you alone.	
9	Pretend to make a phone call to either a friend or the police or	keep your phone hidden.	
10	Where possible, move to a public place or	stay where you are.	
11	If it is someone you know, make it clear that you just don't see them like that or	focus on their feelings because you don't want to harm a friendship.	
12	Stay calm at all times or	if you are feeling angry, show it.	

Part Two – feedback

Go round the Circle and ask pairs to give their response. Ensure that everyone knows the safer option.

1 Use "I" statements to make it clear that you are aware what is happening and taking some control.
2 Ignoring may give missed messages – make your views clear.

3   A smile may encourage the other person; stay neutral.

4   Looking directly at someone gives the impression that you are confident and mean what you say.

5   Speak loudly and clearly so others are aware if they are in the vicinity.

6   Using "I" statements is better and is unambiguous.

7   You don't need an excuse to say no, but if you are feeling unsafe it is better to lie.

8   Stopping to argue means you are not moving to safety – stop what you are doing and move somewhere where there are other people.

9   Your safety is more important than your phone. Use it wisely, even if you have to pretend to call someone.

10 You are safer with other people around – check out the nearest place and move there. If you go into a shop or café, let people there know you are being harassed.

11 Say that you value their friendship but that is as far as it goes. If they persist they are risking the friendship. Do nothing that they might interpret as encouraging, such as responding to texts.

12 You might feel angry and upset – but staying calm is more effective in looking confident and being appropriately assertive.

Upstanding: A bystander watches bullying behaviour and does nothing; an upstander takes action

It is hard for someone to be an upstander on their own. In small groups discuss the following do's and don'ts and how easy or difficult each one is to carry out.

* Don't laugh – hurting or humiliating someone is not a joke.
* Don't join in, but show your disapproval.
* Do not photograph or video the incident to post online – this may backfire against the person being bullied.
* Do tell the person to 'leave it out' or 'leave them alone' – in whatever words you use to stop it.
* Do go and stand by the person being bullied and talk with them – check out how they are.
* Do ask others around to help out to stop this behaviour.
* Report it to someone in authority if it continues.

Use this student-made video, *Stand Up, Stand Strong – the consequence of words*, to generate further discussion on everyone's responsibility to ensure that we are all safe. youtube.com/watch?v=GYYSFpFGRBE&list=PLvzOwE5lWqhScOdC3xMzs9FoAAf pxA-Tz&index=6

Building a Safe and friendly class

Pair share and sentence completion

Pupils are mixed up and then work with a partner to talk about why Safety at school is important and what needs to happen to make sure everyone feels safe. They then complete the sentence going round the Circle:

– "Safety in school means ..."
– "We feel safe in school when ..."

They may need to be reminded that there is no naming or blaming in Circles.

Group Design

Pupils work in groups of three or four to design a safe and friendly school. They are given a large piece of paper that they can draw and write on. Each person in the group contributes. They are asked to show what people would see in a safe and friendly school, what they would hear, and what everyone would be feeling. Each group shows and explains their design to the whole Circle. When everyone has done this, the teacher highlights similarities between them.

Trust

Trust is often an abstract concept, but thinking it through with others in Circles is a way of increasing relational Safety in a school. Spreading these activities over several weeks maintains a focus on the issues raised and builds good practice.

Mix pupils up with these *silent statements*

– Everyone who knows what it means to trust someone change places
– Everyone who knows what it means to be trustworthy change places
– Everyone who thinks that trust is a good thing to have in a relationship change places.

Sentence completions

In pairs pupils discuss how they will finish this sentence stem:

– "*You know you can trust someone when ...*"

They agree on two sentence completions, and each pupil says one of these going round the Circle. It is OK if people say the same things as it shows what everyone thinks. The teacher points out what has been said most often.

Mix pupils up again and ask them to complete these sentences:

– "*Being able to trust other people would make someone feel ...*"
– "*Not being able to trust someone would make someone feel ...*"

Small group discussion

If Trust walked into our school or class tomorrow morning:

- What would we notice? What would be different?
- What might we see, hear, think, and feel?
- What could we do to make sure Trust stays?

Each group has three minutes to tell the rest of the Circle what they would notice and what actions might be needed to increase Trust in their class.

Hypotheticals

A student volunteers to reads out a brief story about a pupil in a particular situation. This is one about someone who is not feeling safe at school. The story is always in the first person, which is fine because it is fictional – though the issues are not. The teacher may need to amend the story so that it does not identify anyone in the class.

My name is Matty. I live with my two mums and little sister who is eight. Most of the time everything is fine, but this year a couple of people in my class have been constantly picking on me, saying horrible things about my family. Recently they have been waiting outside the gates for me and following me home, saying that people like me shouldn't be allowed in school. It is making me miserable and a bit scared.

The pupils work in groups of three or four. They are asked these questions one at a time:

- How would you feel if you were Matty?
- What would you want to happen?
- What is one thing that might help?
- Who will do what when?

Someone from each group comes up to Matty and asks if their action plan is something he would like to happen to help make him safe.

There are many more hypotheticals in *Circle Solutions for Student Wellbeing* 3rd ed (2020), addressing such issues as racism, disability, and children in different families.

Growing good men

This activity is for boys only and best facilitated by a male facilitator.

Part One

Working in groups of three or four, give students the following questions one at a time. Ask for one of the group to record contributions.

What does it mean to be a good man? Imagine what you would like people to say about you at a significant birthday in the future.

What does it mean to be a 'real man' in our society? What is acceptable, what is not? Where are these messages and expectations coming from?

Invite the groups to share their responses and write these up.

Part Two: Silent statements

Ask students to change places if they agree with the following statements:

- Boys and young men are getting confusing messages about how they should be.
- Being a 'tough guy' does not feel comfortable sometimes.
- We have choices about who we become.

Part Three

In different groups of three or four, the students discuss the following:

- Are some boys wearing an imaginary mask to stop others seeing what they really want and need?
- Is it OK for boys to talk about how they feel? What happens when they don't?
- What support do boys need?

Groups feedback responses to the Circle – especially to the last question.

(Taken from Roffey, S. (2020) *Circle Solutions for Student Wellbeing* 3rd ed. Sage.)

Safety checklist

	This is in place – we know it is effective because …	Working on it – our actions to date are …	Just started – our next step will be …
Students' views on how safe they feel at school.			
Staff views on school Safety			
Staff know what to do in a medical emergency			
Mistakes positioned as a necessary step in learning			
Pupil-centred approach to Safety procedures			
Input on e-safety, cyber-bullying, and how to keep everyone safe in a digital world			
A school culture where women and girls are safe and treated with respect			
Pupils encouraged to be 'upstanders' to bullying			
Staff given trauma-informed training			

Safety in the future

Young people are growing up in a world that on one hand is safer than ever before. Child mortality in many countries is much lower than in previous eras, and we have more or less eradicated a number of serious illnesses such as polio, smallpox and diphtheria. But the Covid-19 pandemic shows that without vigilance and collaboration these advances in physical Safety may not be sustainable.

Young people are increasingly unhappy, and for many their emotional Safety is fragile, with more pupils experiencing anxiety, depression and low self-esteem and some resorting to self-harm.

Where parents and carers are stressed by poverty and isolation they may not have the resources to ensure the wellbeing of their families. There are record numbers of children and young people at risk of abuse and neglect, and many witness family conflict and violence even when not hurt themselves. Some are refugees and asylum seekers who have experienced major trauma in their journey to what they hoped would be a kinder place to live. Our students are often not safe.

Safety is also compromised by the growing climate emergency and this generation currently in education is increasingly aware of how negligent the world has been in protecting the planet in favour of economic growth. As the evidence is writ large in heat-waves, fires, floods and storms, we cannot keep young people away from these realities forever, although many try. Although their future Safety is insecure, we can support student wellbeing by giving them Agency to take action and make changes in their own lives and surroundings where they can and learn to be global citizens (see Chapter 1 on Agency).

In school we have the option to ensure that young people are safe to learn and thrive. Many educators are already making a significant difference to students' lives. It starts with the will do to this and the courage to follow through.

References, further reading and resources

Australian National Safe Schools Framework (n.d.). files.eric.ed.gov/fulltext/ED590680.pdf

Department for Education (2018. – updated 2022). *Working Together to Safeguard Children: Statutory Guidance (England).*

Department for Education (2022). *Keeping Children Safe in Education: Statutory Guidance for Schools and Colleges.* Department for Education

Long, R., Robert, N., & Loft, P. (2020). *Bullying in UK Schools, Briefing Paper 8812.* House of Commons Library.

NAPCAN. (n.d.). *Safer Communities for Children.* napcan.org.au/Programs/safer-communities-for-children

Other sources and further reading

Bee, J. (2022). Wellbeing and safeguarding. In K. Evans, T. Hoyle, F. Roberts, & B. Yusuf (Eds), *The Big Book of Whole School Wellbeing.* Corwin.

Booren, L.M., Handy, D.J., & Power, T.G. (2011). Examining perceptions of school safety strategies, school climate, and violence. *Youth Violence and Juvenile Justice, 9*(2), 171–187.

Timmerman, G. (2005). A comparison between girls' and boys' experiences of unwanted sexual behaviour in secondary schools, *Educational Research, 47*(3), 291–306.

Resources

There is a wealth of information on this site, including videos, resources for teachers, and more. This is the link to scenarios to use with students to discuss actions to take. esafety.gov.au/educators/training-for-professionals/professional-learning-program-teachers/inappropriate-content-scenarios

safe4me.co.uk

saferinternet.org.uk/guide-and-resource/young-people/resources-for-11-19s

Stereotypes and prejudice lesson pack – free download: twinkl.co.uk/resource/stereotypes-and-prejudice-lesson-pack-t-p-1643886939

Australian National Safe Schools Framework files.eric.ed.gov/fulltext/ED590680.pdf

esafety.gov.au/key-issues/esafety-guide – this gives information about a range of digital services, games and apps and how young people can protect themselves and others.

raisingchildren.net.au/school-age/behaviour/bullying/school-bullying-helping

anti-bullyingalliance.org.uk

A Call to Men: Tony Porter (TED Talk from 2010) ted.com/talks/tony_porter_a_call_to_men – this is a valuable resource to talk to boys about what Tony Porter calls a 'Man Box'.

3 Positivity
Strengths, solutions, smiles and support

What do we mean by Positivity?

In some ways Positivity has had a bad name. It is sometimes associated with a denial of the difficulties in life, and a Pollyanna view in which everything has a rosy tinge. But Positivity in its many and varied facets has immense benefits for both individual and whole-school wellbeing. It addresses and builds the following:

- Emotional wellbeing
- Self-construct and self-belief
- Values of kindness, consideration and support
- Strengths-based communication
- Positive cognition and mindsets
- Meaningful and uplifting experiences
- Healthy relationships
- Constructive approaches to challenges
- A sense of fun and shared enjoyment.

The default position for many is the negative. People do not always seek to identify what is going well and how to get more of this and opt instead to spend time identifying deficits and dissecting what is wrong. They focus on why things don't work and how to fix them – usually as quickly and as cheaply as possible – often with short-term, unsustainable out-comes. Positivity costs nothing except the belief that it matters and willingness to enact it. It may take more thought, but not necessarily more time or effort, than other ways of being but is undoubtedly more effective in promoting both learning and wellbeing.

This chapter explores how we can build Positivity throughout a school, so that both learners and teachers feel good about being there, the language used is supportive, there is a focus on building healthy relationships and instead of taking problems apart there are solution-focused ways of coping with challenges.

Why does Positivity matter?

Congruence with the United Nations Convention on the Rights of the Child

Article 31 (leisure, play and culture): Every child has the right to relax, play and take part in a wide range of cultural and artistic activities.

DOI: 10.4324/9781003428244-4

Mental health and wellbeing

There is a cohort of young people who rarely feel positive about themselves, other people, or the world around them. They are often swamped with negativity, and their attitudes, sense of self, behaviour, and relationships all reflect this negativity. Positivity in schools has the potential to reverse this when school leaders have the will to initiate action and the belief that it is doable.

Adolescents are particularly vulnerable to mental health concerns. Deteriorating mental health for young people worldwide was the case before the pandemic and has worsened since. Although poverty increases family stress and impacts on positive functioning, economic circumstances are not the only reason students are not doing well. Adverse childhood experiences (ACEs) are clearly a prime cause, but other environmental factors are also involved. These include anxiety about performance in school; worrying about what is happening at home; fear of not being 'good enough', often fuelled by social media; bullying and other social factors; and inconsistent or unsupportive parenting. Mental health difficulties increase with age, with girls more at risk, specifically being worried about appearance, social acceptance, violence in relationships and loneliness. Although some students are brought to the attention of teachers, many more struggle but do not reach criteria for individual intervention. Not only do we need to consider the needs of all vulnerable young people in education but also how to promote wellbeing for all. No-one is exempt from issues that inhibit flourishing. We need to put humour, hope, optimism and kindness at the heart of every school to optimise the potential for a positive trajectory into adulthood.

Healthy relationships

The quality of our relationships is at the crux of our happiness or misery. In schools these comprise peer relationships for both teachers and students, teacher–pupil, staff–executive and parent–school. Although healthy relationships require activation of all the ASPIRE principles, we focus here on Positivity. This includes a ratio of five positive interactions for every negative one. These micro-moments of high-quality interactions build expectations and relationships over time that enhance trust, support and collaboration. Although it is inevitable that at times we need to critique someone's behaviour, attitude or work, if we are also regularly noticing and commenting on their strengths, thanking them for their contributions and showing belief in the best of them, it is easier for that individual to listen to and accept criticism. They are less likely to be devastated by a negative comment if their sense of self has been fortified and they do not feel so vulnerable.

Relationships are actioned by what is said and not said, and messages that are given about how we value someone. This includes interest, gratitude, generosity, acceptance, respect and courtesy.

Positive thinking

Inner discourse

How we think about ourselves, other people, and situations that happen to us can either be predominantly negative or mostly positive. A pessimistic outlook is sometimes thought of as more realistic, but it can also lead to self-fulfilling expectations that can be harmful. Optimism, on the other hand, has links to better physical health, including longevity, coping skills, creativity, constructive problem-solving and positive social interactions. Raising awareness of inner dialogue, the options available and the value of positive choices is worthwhile.

Solution-focused

Rather than focusing on a problem, solution-focused thinking begins with what you want to achieve. When you have a vision of what a situation would look like with the difficulties resolved, you are then able to consider steps towards that goal. You identify what is already in place, what has worked well in the past, and what resources, skills and strategies you have at your disposal. You might then identify what else you might need and how others might help. This is often used for individuals in therapy but is also applicable to organisations such as schools. When school leaders identify a clear vision for their school, they can be more confident of the policies and processes developed to action this. It is OK to begin with the ideal even if you never get there – you at least know where you are heading.

Growth mindset

A fixed mindset is where someone believes they either have innate ability or they don't. A growth mindset is acknowledging that effort, persistence, good strategies and support can make all the difference to achievement. When students hear that they are 'clever' or 'good at maths', they will be devastated when they do not do well, as this undermines who they believe they are. They may also blame others rather than evaluate their own efforts. A growth mindset is promoted by encouraging young people to see that the more resources put into something the more successful this is likely to be. Carol Dweck (2017) has updated her views on growth mindset to say that it is not only effort that matters but a wide range of strategies to unlock learning.

Constructive problem-solving

Although intelligence can be a protective factor for mental health, it can also make things worse. This happens when someone thinks of all the things that could go wrong, imagines the breadth and depth of potential disasters and catastrophises. The positioning of difficulties as challenges rather than overwhelming obstacles, however, can reduce anxiety and the tendency to 'negatively ruminate'. There are always options in any given situation, including doing nothing. Constructive problem-solving is a skill that can be taught. All students would benefit from learning what this entails. It includes brainstorming possible options in response to a challenge and then reflecting on the pros and cons of each, including both inner and outer resources available. The penultimate stage is choosing one to try and another as backup, and the final stage is checking whether any strategy needs tweaking to be more effective (see L.A.T.E.R. in Chapter 5 on Respect). Constructive problem-solving not only engages creativity and courage but also reduces the power of negative emotions, especially feelings of helplessness.

The language of strengths

The words that individuals hear about themselves influence their self-concept, especially if the people using them are significant in their lives – parents, extended family, carers and teachers. If we regularly tell teenagers they are lazy, selfish or irresponsible, that is how they will think of themselves and live up to these expectations. Helping young people identify their strengths – not just abilities – can be a powerful antidote to this. Although Seligman's VIA strengths (Petersen & Seligman, 2004) framework is now used widely, there are many more expressed in simple language that also extend possibilities. This alternative framework might be useful. You can, of course, add more (Table 3.1).

Table 3.1 Strengths

Interpersonal strengths	Resilience strengths	Ethical strengths	Personal strengths	Other strengths
friendly	thankful	responsible	creative	sporting
willing to share	optimistic	honest	adventurous	musical
warm	keeps things in perspective	trustworthy	hard-working	artistic
caring	determined	fair	neat and tidy	imaginative
good listener	cheerful	acknowledges mistakes	sense of humour	graceful
helpful	sets goals	can make amends	energetic	good with animals
supportive	adaptable	respects confidentiality	enthusiastic	relaxed
fun to be with	inclusive	reliable	thoughtful	can fix things
considerate	can change	democratic	confident	colourful
interested	positive	asks questions	courageous	independent
kind	assertive	forgiving	careful	team player
empathic	problem-solver	non judgmental	curious	organised

(From Roffey, 2011)

The value of a strengths approach

Adopting a strengths focus in schools can positively shape personal wellbeing, relationships, and school culture. Human beings are hardwired to pay attention to threat and danger, and that is especially the case if we have experienced this before. We are good at noticing what's wrong, but tend to overlook or not notice what's going right. We believe we see the full picture, but attention is more like a laser beam than a floodlight, so when we are fully focused on what's not working, we may miss seeing what is going well. In schools, that is a disadvantage for building positive relationships as well as for learning and problem-solving.

- Knowing the negatives about someone tells you nothing about their positive qualities.
- It's easier to feel connected to someone who notices what's good about you than with someone who only points out your flaws or errors.
- The seeds of a solution to any problem lie in what's working, not in what's broken.

Adopting a strengths focus is an effective way of compensating for an ingrained negativity bias. It means learning to pay attention to the many ways that things do go right and the positives that people bring to a situation.

The simplest description of a personal strength is something you do well and enjoy. Because people enjoy using their strengths, it is helpful to watch out for the things that people are eager to do and energised by doing. Every student and teacher needs to know their strengths so they can use and build on them. Individuals who know and use their strengths are much more likely to have a higher level of wellbeing than those who don't. Strength awareness is also associated with greater engagement, self-efficacy, and wellbeing. We feel better about ourselves when we focus on the things we do well and enjoy doing. This increased engagement and self-efficacy can unlock virtuous learning cycles.

Positive emotions

Negative emotions are diverse and have numerous expressions. Emotions such as anger, fear and disgust have a protective role in reacting rapidly to threat: emotional memory and circumstance combine to trigger the amygdala – the organ in the limbic system of the brain – leading to responses of flight, fight or freeze: run away fast, attack or pretend you're not there. It is usually when students perceive a threat – usually to their sense of self – that they react in ways that can be hard to manage (see Chapter 2 on Safety). Note that it is the perception of threat that matters, not whether it consists of real danger or not.

Unsurprisingly it has been negative emotions that have been the historical focus of research. The role of positive emotions has only received attention since the end of the twentieth century and the increasing interest in positive psychology. Although there are many and varied ways of feeling positive, they do not have the wide variety of expression that negative emotions do, because they do not activate responses in the same way. Some researchers have made a distinction between the definition of emotions and the definition of feelings. Emotions are embodied responses to stimuli, experienced physiologically, whereas feelings are subjective responses to how someone might interpret what is happening. We will, however, use the terms interchangeably here.

Positive psychology has made explicit what most teachers have known forever, that when learners are full of anxiety, depression and fear they do not function so well in the classroom. Positive feelings, on the other hand, open up cognitive pathways and promote both creativity and problem-solving abilities. Fredrickson's 'broaden and build theory' (2001, 2013) suggests that positive emotions help us stay focused and expand our thinking, offering more options and strategies. They also undo the cardiovascular effects of negative emotions. Both support coping skills in the face of adversity. Positive feelings include feeling well, being interested, being comfortable, having fun, feeling a sense of pride, being connected with others, having hope and optimism, and feeling acknowledged and valued. The following illustrates some ways in which positive emotions might be strengthened within the learning environment.

Play

Although play and playfulness enhance positive emotions, this is rarely seen as worthy of attention in secondary education. Unless aligned with sports, play is positioned as more relevant to younger children. But adolescents are often immersed in video games and when given the opportunity to play face to face may choose to engage in playful, imaginative and explorative interaction.

Free play and interaction are how many of us learn to solve problems, discover and develop interests, have autonomy and build a wide range of competencies. Freedom to play has declined greatly in recent decades. Adult-directed and -monitored activities for young people have increased, with more time in school than ever before, and greatest significance given to success in academic subjects. Activities outside of school are also largely directed and controlled by adults. This may inhibit the development of creativity, innovation, and a positive sense of self.

Peter Gray (2011) researched the impact of reducing free play and found a correlation between the decline of play and the rise in mental ill health. Play builds resilience, helps traumatised young people to adapt and cope, and decreases stress. Learning through challenges that play presents is fun and rewarding. Adventure playgrounds are useful for all ages, including teenagers, who often enjoy taking physical challenges in a controlled environment – a bit like a fairground.

When young people are playing freely and making their own choices either alone or with others, they are interacting with the environment on their own terms, exploring, and discovering with all their senses. With no adult-directed agenda, it is possible to be creative, inventive, imaginative and self-reliant. This builds understanding, stimulates questions and promotes cognitive development generally.

Teenagers may say they are bored if they are not offered activities on a plate and look to adults to provide entertainment. Boredom, however, can be the stimulus to discover what they can do for themselves. Unfortunately, many may resort to passive entertainment on screens rather than active engagement with the environment. Limiting screen time is a discussion many adults are now having. There are also fewer resources for young people in the community, especially in impoverished areas of the UK.

Playfulness

Play is not the same as playfulness: in educational settings playfulness boosts both positive behaviour and engagement in learning (Johnston et al., 2023). Students say that they value teachers who find ways to make lessons fun. Playfulness is a way of injecting humour, warmth and connection into the classroom – fostering the positive emotions that enhance learning, memory and a sense of belonging. It is an approach to building a specific classroom culture. Playful learning is more 'hands-on' and less didactic. It encourages exploration of a subject with others. It is where teachers find examples to illustrate their teaching that have elements of surprise or unusual application. It can be where teachers position themselves as learners alongside their students and share the excitement of discovering something new.

Humour is protective. People who can see the funny side of life's mishaps are likely to interpret and react to stress more positively, buffering themselves against some of the negative effects. Laughing releases oxytocin, thought to make us less likely to ruminate on or re-experience stressful events. It also helps to build positive relationships, providing the social support that is key to healthy adolescent development.

Creativity

There is increasing concern in the UK about the dilution of creativity in schools alongside significant cuts to arts funding in universities. With more focus on STEM (science, technology, engineering and maths) the importance of imaginative, innovative and artistic endeavours has been downplayed. This is particularly critical in state education where subjects that appeal to many young people and may lift their spirits are no longer available to many. Creativity is needed more than ever to address mental health issues but also has the potential to encourage disaffected young people to stay in school.

> *Sport, music, drama, art, debating and dance should be an integral part of the timetable for all children, not an optional 'extra-curricular' add-on.*
>
> (Sylvester & Seldon, 2022)

Positivity in practice in the secondary classroom

The New South Wales Commission for Children and Young People (2002–2009) asked students to say what they thought characterised a good teacher. The responses included that a teacher tries to make learning fun, that they 'smile at me', and 'ask me how I'm doing but not just in school'.

Teacher–student relationships

There is now a wealth of evidence confirming that the quality of the relationship between teacher and student makes a significant difference to learning outcomes. This includes getting to know something about each pupil at the beginning of the school year. Educators can then utilise this information to show interest and appreciation that build positive relationships and the ability to more effectively support engagement with learning. This saves time later on picking up the pieces when things go awry.

Relationships are built in the thousands of micro-moments that take place in the classroom every day. Choosing the positive takes no more time and effort than defaulting to the negative. Here is an acronym that might help:

Going WALKIES

WELCOME students, look pleased to see them, using their name if you can remember it and asking them to remind you if you can't.

ACKNOWLEDGE their presence, efforts and achievements – not just in work but in character and strength development.

LISTENING is hard for busy teachers, but 20 seconds of full attention can enable a pupil to feel heard. Social and emotional learning in Circle Solutions gives opportunities for every student to speak even if briefly.

KINDNESS is both in the things we do and in the words we say. Teacher wellbeing is essential so that responses stay thoughtful and not knee-jerk reactions to stressful situations.

INVITATION either to participate with others or for their opinion, shows that someone matters.

ENTHUSIASM is a great gift for an educator – and can be contagious, making it easier to engage students. Being enthusiastic about students themselves and their efforts can also bring benefits.

SMILING is a universal and powerful indicator of friendliness and connection. Regularly smiling at students lifts everyone up and generates a culture of warmth across a class.

SILENCES – there are times when it is important to say something and times when words can make something worse. Much of the time a criticism is redundant – the person already knows they messed up, they don't need others to tell them.

Adults apologising when they have been angry or irritable, get something wrong, or jump to conclusions without checking facts, provide a strong role model for students who might appreciate this self-awareness and honesty. It also shows that no-one loses face by taking responsibility, and that imperfection is part of all of us.

The words of a teacher are powerful. They can create dreams or crush them. Belief in a young person and their potential builds a positive sense of self and is the root of resilience and the driver of wellbeing.

Teaching and learning

The vast majority of students in the US are engaged at school when they start but become increasingly disengaged with learning; only 37% have any enthusiasm by the time they leave (Jenkins, 2019). Around a quarter of Danish students are often bored at school (Knoop et al., 2016), and this figure is replicated internationally. In the Times Education Commission Report (Sylvester & Seldon, 2022) Nobel prize-winning geneticist Paul Nurse says *"you don't excite people with lots and lots of facts … Textbooks get thicker and thicker and ideas get thinner and thinner … we need to excite people with ideas and understanding."*

So how might positivity impact on teaching and learning? How might we move students along the trajectory from the negative emotions of boredom and disaffection to the positive emotions of interest, enthusiasm and even excitement in the classroom? This is a simple summary of some of the positive strategies identified in the literature:

- Promoting curiosity – presenting students with something that connects to their own lives and builds on prior knowledge but encourages new perspectives. When teaching is primarily knowledge transmission we risk under-estimating student potential for building on their own experience, and the deep learning that may result from this.
- Using stories, videos and other internet resources. There is now a wealth of material available that has the potential to stimulate interest.
- One way of beginning a lesson is to position something as a mystery to be solved. Good questions are valuable in engaging adolescent minds that are developing abstract thinking skills.
- Experiencing and exploring – students are more engaged with hands-on activities.
- Activities such as mind-maps, debates and podcasts reinforce curricula outcomes.
- Sharing and reflecting – paired discussions lead to more engagement and deeper learning. These discussions can focus on a range of issues:

  - Devising questions about the material to further their understanding
  - Researching answers to questions posed by the teacher
  - Transferring understanding to novel situations – generalising knowledge
  - Exploring how new knowledge might be applied or developed.

Project- or problem-based collaborative learning is more engaging for students. It gives young people agency, is non-competitive, and addresses real-world issues that make education more meaningful. Read more about this and also 'flipped learning' in Chapter 1 on Agency.

Positivity in practice across the secondary school

Playfulness diffuses conflict and creates connection. A playful teacher sets the tone for a peaceful, positive-emotion fuelled classroom, moving beyond the need to rely on operant behaviour management systems or power dynamics.

(Tidmund, 2021)

It is hard for teachers to be light-hearted and playful in an environment where they are under great pressure to deliver high academic outcomes. They may also have less tolerance for pupils who are not focused, compliant or achieving. It is not only sad but dangerous when negativity dominates, as this can result in a toxic school culture. There are many schools across the world operating in a healthy positive way that supports everyone with their learning. This does not mean ignoring problematic issues, but ensuring that both students and teachers feel good about being there, and that the culture is warm and supportive and as far as possible learning is joyful.

A teacher once told me that, although they were obliged to carry out the national tests that everyone was mandated to do, the senior leadership team at her school were determined they would not be the focus of conversation or classroom practice for weeks beforehand. This showed staff they had confidence in their teaching. The tests came and went, and results were on a par with others. Wellbeing was the priority, and anxiety kept at a minimum.

Playfulness

Playfulness is creative, fun and allows teachers to be in charge of proceedings without controlling learners. A light-hearted approach both engages students and has the potential to reduce anxiety. Laughing together increases a sense of belonging. There are many ways to do this. Teachers can make fun of themselves to good effect. It is valuable when teachers own a mistake – sometimes a deliberate one – as it gives permission for pupils to take risks with their learning.

It is not only young people who benefit from playfulness. When this is promoted across an organisation it also boosts the wellbeing of adults. Experiencing positive emotions has the same outcomes for teachers as for students, for engagement and learning. With individuals it can also enhance motivation and meaning. Playfulness with others can generate aspects of positive relationships, such as trust and collaboration.

Oxytocin is the neurotransmitter released in many reproductive activities. This promotes connection, bonding, trust and cooperation. It is also released when people laugh together. This is worth doing both in the classroom and the staffroom and can have a positive impact on school culture overall.

While there are few documented examples of playfulness in practice within staff environments, recent research into playfulness amongst adults in the work environment found evidence that specific playful practices could improve wellbeing and reduce symptoms of depression (Proyer et al., 2021). This included noticing and recording playful moments during a day, seeking opportunities at work to be playful and focusing on how this made people feel and keeping count of the moments in which employees either participated or witnessed playful interactions, jokes or even just doing something differently to raise a laugh. Although these practices were only carried out for a week there were positive impacts on wellbeing up to 12 weeks later. Playful practices might include the following:

- Dress up days – characters from films, history or popular culture
- Lunchtime karaoke – with staff as well as students
- Fashion parades with unclaimed lost property
- Something unexpected and humorous over the public address system
- Themed weeks such as those described below
- Limerick competitions
- Team scavenger hunts – perhaps linked to curriculum content
- Funny photo competitions
- Team quizzes and games

Parents and community members might be asked to contribute to some of these ideas but would need to know the importance of promoting positivity for wellbeing in the first instance.

Positive Pathway

Murals don't always have to be on a wall. This creative initiative was taken by the Aboriginal Girls Circle in Delroy School, Dubbo College.

We decided on POSITIVITY for a themed week. This included the whole school being involved in different activities throughout the week (e.g. staff versus student sport, trivia, colour days).

- We decided to fund raise for the mental health charity Beyond Blue
- We advertised the positive pathway through our Wellbeing lessons, inviting students to submit a draft copy of anything positive that they would like to see on the pathway (e.g. phrases, pictures, words, images, colours)
- Students then submitted their drafts to the Girls Circle for us to check spelling etc
- We then sent notes out to all students and staff who submitted their draft to congratulate them on being part of the Positive Pathway mural
- On the day students and staff assembled on the back oval and chose a part of the pathway they wanted to paint
- It took all day to paint the pathway, but staff and students had a great time
- The pathway was vibrant and colourful. It included simple statements such as 'smile', 'be positive' and 'be strong and be brave', and also paintings of rainbows, trees and handprints
- On this day Girls Circle also made blue cupcakes, did face painting and raised about $2,000 for Beyond Blue
- Local press were contacted and wrote a feature on Positive Pathways with photos.

Strengths across a school

A strengths approach goes beyond the benefits to individuals – it has much wider benefits in that it builds relationships and transforms group culture. Strengths spotting is the name commonly given to the practice of noticing and commenting on strengths in others. It is the practice that unlocks the relational power of the strengths approach. When teachers focus on noticing what's going well with students, situations, and their own teaching, this has the potential to transform the culture in which they work and learn.

The power of a strengths approach for building a positive school culture

The research I conducted with students and their teachers in primary and intermediate schools in New Zealand demonstrated the relational and cultural power of the strengths approach. Through a classroom-based programme, students learned about their strengths and were encouraged to notice strengths in others. They practiced strengths spotting in class, peer to peer, and teachers were encouraged to notice strengths in students.

These practices improved student wellbeing, behavioural and emotional engagement in the classroom, and connectedness between students. They improved class social climate through increased cohesion and less friction. Several teachers independently reported that there was less teasing and bullying in their classrooms. One teacher noted that students not only were more accepting of each other, they were now protective of their classmates in the wider school playground.

Results from this study also demonstrated the powerful role that teachers play in influencing classroom behaviour. The positive outcomes were directly driven (mediated in statistical terms) by teacher behaviour. Where teachers reported higher levels of strengths spotting in their students, students reported greater benefits from the programme. This finding suggests that the role of teachers in strengths programmes is pivotal for their success. Where teachers are supportive of and engage with strengths practices, including role modelling and strengths spotting, students are more likely to adopt these practices, including in peer-to-peer relationships.

Dr Denise Quinlan, Director, New Zealand Institute of Resilience and Wellbeing

Kindness

No act of kindness, however small, is ever wasted.

—Aesop

An act of kindness is a generous, deliberate gesture or action directed towards another person, animal, or the planet. It is altruistic and does not expect reciprocity. Random acts of kindness cost nothing, but not every young person knows what this is, nor understands how it not only helps others, but boosts their own positive feelings too (Otake et al., 2006). We are neurologically primed to help others. Being kind boosts serotonin and dopamine, which are neurotransmitters that promote feelings of satisfaction and wellbeing and cause the pleasure/reward centres in the brain to light up.

Kindness UK have sent out nearly 5,000 free packs to secondary schools to show teachers how to incorporate kindness into their teaching. They also give out a Kind School of the Year Award.

Kindness week in Westhoughton High School in Lancashire

The school had a kindness week at the end of term. Each year group raised money for their chosen charity on one set day. Staff did one lesson on the theme of kindness. Highlights were wellie walks and wellie-wanging for Give Hunger the Boot, and random acts of kindness by the school council kindness army when they went around the local community giving away sweets and flowers and washing cars for free. As well as raising money for charity the overall impression was that school culture itself was enriched.

Some comments from staff:

- "All round great week which really showed the kindness of all pupils and staff."
- "I thought Kindness Week was absolutely brilliant! It has been one of the most enjoyable weeks I have experienced in school!"
- "What a fantastic idea of having the kindness postcards – I have really enjoyed the kind comments sent from pupils, who have really made my week."

Some comments from students:

- "I loved making kindness cards for staff and my friends."
- "My highlight was people complimenting me."
- "The concert was fantastic."
- "I like Kindness lessons."

Some comments from the community:

- *"You've really made my day."*
- *"We should have more of this!"*
- *"What a brilliant idea!"*

The Kindness Matters Campaign

UNESCO Mahatma Gandhi Institute of Education for Peace and Sustainable Development's (MGIEP's) #KindnessMatters Campaign aims to mobilize young people to carry out transformative acts of kindness to tackle the Sustainable Development Goals and create a positive culture of kindness. So far 5,095,307 acts of kindness have been recorded in this initiative. A kindness wall in school might encourage students to identify stories in the media that illustrate the many ways that kindness might be enacted and to record their own contributions to this campaign.

Positive thinking

Optimism

Optimistic thinking is where someone anticipates positive outcomes but also has cognitive strategies that stop them being overwhelmed when things do not go to plan. It is the opposite of the learned helplessness that Martin Seligman says is at the root of depression. He has written about both (Petersen et al., 1995; Seligman, 2006). Optimism is hope for the future, and can be encouraged in school by the conversations that take place. The word 'yet' is particularly valuable, as in *"You haven't quite understood that yet"*. This shows that learning is on a trajectory and that there is still some way to go. Optimistic thinking may require some reframing of a situation to avoid catastrophising. Normalising a difficult event can help put things into perspective, e.g. *"These things happen sometimes, let's just clear up the mess"* or *"You did not do well in that test, but it's not the end of the world, maybe you will do better next time"*.

Gratitude

When gratitude permeates school culture it generates multiple positive outcomes. It can be defined in three ways: a feeling of thankfulness, an appreciative thought, and acknowledgement in action. Here we focus on the little things that schools might do to build positive relationships by showing gratitude. In some places this is harder than others as, like most things, gratitude is driven by context. But modelling gratitude alongside other positive ways of being can be contagious. The more it happens, the more likely it will become embedded.

With students

- All staff are encouraged to recognise any effort that students have made. For some just getting to school in the morning is an achievement.

- Over time ask pupils to find out about the roles of different people who work in the school, such as the cleaner, the caretaker and the school admin staff. What do they do? When do they do it? What difference does this make to how the school runs? They then write thank-you notes, perhaps making the letters specific for things that matter most to them. In one school a class left a bunch of flowers or a bar of chocolate for the cleaner from time to time. Their classroom was especially sparkly!
- Ask students to think of one thing they learnt that day they found interesting and share this with a partner.

With families

- Position families as experts on their child and thank them for sharing their knowledge with you.
- Thank people for coming to meetings, especially parents for whom it might be a struggle.
- Both in writing reports and in meetings, begin with the positive about the student. Say what they have achieved, the strengths they have demonstrated, and something about them that you value/like. This does several things. It shows you have that student's best interests at heart. It promotes positive and trusting relationships, and it means that if you have something difficult to discuss later on, families will be more willing to listen.

With staff

- Putting affirmations in staff pigeon-holes can lift their day and make them feel appreciated. This is not necessarily about good work but about the personal qualities they bring to the job.
- In whole-school Circle Solutions training I have sometimes asked everyone to tape a piece of paper on their back and then all staff to write on the paper what they value about them as a colleague, usually limiting this to ten statements, each numbered. The last person takes the paper, folds it into four and gives it to their colleague. The activity only ends when everyone has the requisite ten statements. Staff are then asked to sit back in the Circle, open their paper all together, and read what has been said about them. They are asked to reflect on:
  - What this makes them feel about themselves and the day they are having.
  - What this makes them feel about the colleagues they work with who have written positive things.
  - What this makes them understand about some of the pupils they teach.

Some teachers have said that this brief activity changed how they felt about teaching in the school and gained valuable insight about their relationships with both colleagues and pupils.

- In one secondary school in London, every morning begins with a 5- to 10-minute staff briefing by one of the leadership team. This informs everyone of anything specific happening that day (including staff birthdays), gives any positive feedback (however small) from parents, governors or community, and reports on specific student achievements. This means the day starts with shared good news and people feeling appreciated.
- Some schools have introduced a Random Act of Kindness Board in the staffroom. This is where individuals can put up post-it notes to thank someone for going out of their way to inform, share, offer, support or simply show empathy for someone having a hard time. It applies to everyone in the school and is cleared on a regular basis so there are opportunities for new starts.

Behaviour

It is not the young people whose lives are going well who present the greatest challenges to teachers, but those who are struggling with a wide range of issues, including trauma, loss and anxiety. Schools cannot expect to promote positive behaviour in students by making them feel even worse than they do already. It is more helpful to begin with positioning behaviour as distressed rather than deliberately difficult and replacing authoritarian relationships with facilitative ones that mirror the most effective parenting style – warm, accepting and respectful alongside high expectations for pro-social behaviour.

Addressing all the principles throughout this book will contribute to better behaviour in school, so it is not a question of devising quick-fix strategies but of a universal approach that determines the quality of interactions throughout the school day and across the school.

The more attention you give to unwanted behaviour the more it will dominate. It is better to focus on, acknowledge and build behaviours that promote the positive. This means talking about what is expected, liaising with students to build school culture, having clear routines, giving reminders rather than reprimands and regularly acknowledging positive interactions and effort – the ratio of five positives to every negative. For example:

- "*I like the way you ...*"
- "*Thank you for ...*"
- "*I have noticed that ...*"
- "*I wonder if ...*"
- "*Well done for ...*".

Several 'positive behaviour for learning' initiatives have been adopted in schools. But although the emphasis is on raising the focus on what is expected, they often resort to rewards and sanctions to reinforce this rather than a more relational and agentic approach which changes behaviour 'from the inside out' and builds responsibility over time.

This does not mean that unacceptable behaviour is ignored. A conversation that shows a young person you have belief in the best of them and asks how they are going to repair the damage they have caused gives them a second chance. It is also worth having solution-focused conversations, asking "*What did you want to happen?*" and "*What might have been a better way of getting there?*" Asking students what they feel when they have achieved something, especially if it has been complex or difficult, or demonstrated a strength, will help them realise that certain ways of being are more likely to make them feel good about themselves.

The way teachers speak with students, especially those who are having a tough time, can make more difference than they realise.

> *I had a hard time at home and at school and this one teacher made a real difference for me. He showed he cared whether I was there or not, whether I learned anything. He didn't give up on me. It is because of him that I stayed in school.*

(trainee teacher)

See the section on *Behaviour and restorative practice* in Chapter 4 on Inclusion.

Many schools are now exploring trauma-informed approaches. This is changing expectations, responses and relationships, but it needs whole-school support for those staff who bear a heavy emotional load working with students who have experienced trauma and/or high levels of adversity.

Solution-focused meetings

In some secondary schools all those who teach a student with social, emotional or behavioural issues meet together ostensibly to discuss ways forward. Some of these meetings are, however, opportunities for a moan-fest – spending the available time discussing the last dreadful thing that the student did and how they have all 'tried everything' to no avail. Although this might be cathartic for stressed teachers and seen as supportive, it is not ultimately helpful for either teachers or students – things are unlikely to get better. It may, however, be the precursor to exclusion from mainstream school for the student, especially if they are not contributing to a school's reputation for academic 'excellence'.

A solution-focused meeting would instead be asking the following questions:

- What, if anything, has worked well in the past?
- What are the exceptions to problematic behaviour? Are there times when the student is engaged positively (a) with others or (b) with learning tasks? What is happening at that time? What are the circumstances?
- Have they responded positively, however minimally, to any approach?
- Is there anyone in the student's life who believes in the best of them or with whom they have a supportive relationship? Have there been any conversations with that person to share ideas?
- What strengths does the student have that might be developed in school?
- Do they have any interests that might be helpful in promoting engagement?
- Has anyone tried anything suggested in the last meeting? Was this just once or regularly? Doing something once is like putting cake mix in an oven for five minutes and expecting to get cakes! Positive strategies need to be put in place consistently over time.

It is useful to acknowledge what might have been happening for the student in order to have some empathic understanding of why their behaviour has been challenging. This may avoid an authoritarian approach that is likely to make things worse.

Staff wellbeing

In countries such as Finland teachers are held in high regard, given professional autonomy, and paid well. There is strong competition to enter the profession, with about one in ten applicants being successful. Higher teacher wellbeing is associated with effectiveness and improved student outcomes, retention, resilience, and job satisfaction. Teacher retention is a concern in many countries as stress and burnout take their toll, with experienced educators leaving the profession and possible recruits lacking the motivation to join. Research indicates that in the UK teachers consider their wellbeing lower than that of most other professions, including in health, social work, finance and human resources (Grenville-Cleave & Boniwell, 2012). Teacher mental health is undermined by increased demands for accountability, frequent innovations, an inflexible imposed curriculum, high workload, and insufficient time to establish the teacher–student relationships that bring the greatest satisfaction to the role. Staff absence leads to inconsistent and fragmented teaching, and this in turn impacts on both wellbeing and learning for students. It makes sense for every school to promote teacher wellbeing as an essential feature of whole-school wellbeing.

Staff wellbeing is a multi-dimensional construct that incorporates personal approaches and systemic interventions. Interestingly, levels of burnout do not seem to be related to school socio-economic context, as teachers may be doing well in areas of disadvantage where their job is highly challenging, and choosing to leave more privileged schools whose culture is toxic. What matters is what is going on in schools to support staff. Teachers are often asked to look after their own wellbeing by actions such as taking exercise, getting enough sleep, and finding time to relax with friends and family, but that will be insufficient if organisational expectations and processes are not aligned. Here is a summary of the positive school factors associated with higher teacher wellbeing:

- A supportive and positive school climate and school leaders who generate this
- Caring social relationships and collaboration where teachers support each other and work together
- Shared vision and values
- A professional setting that encourages quality teaching
- Support for autonomy
- Positive teacher–student relationships that provide meaning
- Support from mentors which is of particular relevance for early-career teachers
- Basic structures such as good staffroom facilities, sufficient break-times, scheduling only necessary meetings, and clear expectations for when staff are available and not.

Activity: Secret Angels

Every member of staff who wants to be involved in this initiative puts their name in a hat at the beginning of term. They then take out the name of someone else. They will be the 'secret angel' for this colleague. Their role is to check in with them from time to time, make them the occasional tea or coffee, put a card or cookie in their pigeonhole, perhaps take a duty for them, or celebrate their birthday if they have one during the term. The important thing is that teachers have each other's backs and are there for each other when times are tough.

Workload

No-one can do everything to a high standard of excellence all the time and stay mentally well. The pressure is too great. This applies to both teachers and pupils. School leaders need to work with staff to decide priorities and what can be completed to a level that is acceptable but not consistently 'outstanding'. It is the difference between writing a page of useful and relevant bullet points in a report and writing four pages of prose that takes most of a weekend.

Accountability

Teachers feel demoralised when their own professional judgment is not trusted, their experience/teaching skills undermined, and a restrictive curriculum together with uninspiring teaching methods take the 'excitement' and pleasure out of teaching (DfE, 2018). There has been a rising criticism of school inspections in the UK, the way these are sometimes carried out, and the impact on teacher mental health. People talk about the importance of 'standards' without clarifying what these actually mean for an education fit for the 21st century. Hopefully, by the time this book is published, things will have changed, though the lack of respect for educators has already taken its toll on the profession.

Positivity in social and emotional learning (SEL)

One of the main reasons that Circle Solutions works well, and students regularly ask for it, is that they have fun. Many of the activities in Circles are presented as games, and some of these have no other purpose than to generate laughing together. Young people who have a good time together in Circles are more likely to be friendly and supportive outside the Circle. Some also learn that having fun does not have to be at the expense of others (Hromek & Roffey 2009). Positivity is also demonstrated by focusing on solutions rather than problems.

Activities in SEL

Strengths in Circles Cards

There are seven statements for each of the six ASPIRE principles.
   These are three of those for Positivity:

* We laugh together
* We notice what we have achieved
* We explore possibilities
* We want the best for each other.

In groups of three or four, students take one statement at a time and discuss the following questions together:

– What does this mean?
– Is this what we want in our school?
– What would it make people feel about being here?
– Is it already happening – how do we know?
– What else might we do?
– What help might we need?

Each group decides on one action. They give a brief report back to the Circle, emphasising the action. What they all agree on is put on display as a reminder.

Strengths Identification

1   Play a game that randomly mixes students up. Spread strength cards or photos in the centre of the Circle. Ask each person to pick up a card that represents a strength that they have noticed in their partner and then tell each other why they have chosen this.
2   Spread strength cards, photos or symbols cards in the centre of the Circle. Ask each person to pick up a card that represents a strength they have developed in the last year. They discuss this with a partner.
3   Again using stimulus cards, ask each student to pick up a card that represents a strength that they would like to develop in the coming year.

Positive thinking skills

Mindfulness

Mindfulness is focusing on the present moment, the bodily sensations you are experiencing, and being objective about thoughts and feelings. This helps to reduce fretting about the past or worrying about the future. Mindful breathing, visualisations, or immersing yourself in music are three ways of introducing mindfulness to teenagers. They could also be asked to think of all the times they might have a moment to increase awareness of the now – such as being in a queue, standing in a lift, or waiting for toast to cook. What might they listen to, watch out for, or pay attention to in these moments?

Blessings

Having a positive mindset focuses on what is going well rather than mistakes, imperfections and disasters. There is evidence to show that this staves off depression. It therefore makes sense to boost this thankfulness mentality where possible, making students aware of what they do have. It also helps in reducing a sense of entitlement and promotes empathy for those who have fallen on hard times.

Count your Blessings

Everyone wanders around in the middle of the Circle and at a given signal partners with the person nearest to them – or forms a group of three. The first time they have a conversation about what they are thankful for this week – anything that has gone well. Ensure there is enough time for all pupils to speak if they wish. They then mix up again, and at a second signal they find a new partner or group. This time they talk about something they have been pleased about this year. Finally, after mixing up again, they talk with a new partner or group about something that they are grateful for in their life generally, such as being able to listen to music or having a pet.

Voices

We have different voices in our heads, some of which are more helpful to us than others. This activity divides statements up about an upcoming exam. Ask students to work with a partner and decide which is helpful and which is not. They can then be asked to come up with new statements for each and share these with the rest of the Circle.

Statement	Helpful	Unhelpful
"My mind will go blank."		
"I must remember to read the question carefully."		
"They will ask me something I don't know."		
"Everyone will think I am a loser."		
"Most of my friends will be feeling the same as me."		
"I will just do my best."		
"I haven't revised enough."		
"It's OK not to be the best at everything."		

Positivity checklist

	This is in place – we know it is effective because …	Working on it – our actions to date are …	Just started – our next step will be …
Strengths-based approach			
Solution-focused conversations			
Focus on teacher wellbeing			
Positive actions – kindness, gratitude, playfulness			
Positive relationships			
Constructive communications			
Social-emotional learning that includes awareness of inner discourse, mindfulness, and having fun together			

Positivity in the future

When the media and many soap operas focus on the negative and headlines routinely announce the worst of human behaviour, there is a risk that people will begin to believe that this is the norm. They perceive 'human nature' as greedy, selfish, aggressive, and doom-laden. This can lead to suspicion of others, expectation that we will be treated badly, and a temptation to get in first. This is a recipe for misery and mayhem, and we can already see elements of this on social media, if not in public and political arenas.

But reality paints a different picture. Cruelty and callousness are not the most common ways of being, because when it comes to psychological stability, let alone survival, we need each other. There are plenty of examples – and evidence – that many individuals are kind, considerate, honourable, generous, empathic and grateful for the good things – especially for the healthy, supportive relationships that are at the heart of wellbeing.

We might be forgiven for thinking that altruism and other positive social values are going out of fashion, but they are as relevant to wellbeing as they have ever been. Perhaps for our children to thrive and experience a hopeful future these values need to be brought out into the light and become more central in education. Positivity in all its diverse manifestations needs to colour our conversations, be threaded through our actions, and celebrated in as many spheres as possible, especially in every classroom, every day.

References, further reading and resource

DfE (2018). *Factors Affecting Teacher Retention. A Qualitative Investigation. Research Report.* CooperGibson Research.

Dweck, C.S. (2017). *Mindset – Updated Edition: Changing the Way You think to Fulfil Your Potential.* Random House.

Fredrickson, B.L. (2001). The role of positive emotions in positive psychology. The broaden-and-build theory of positive emotions. *American Psychologist, 56*(3), 218–226.

Fredrickson, B.L. (2013). Positive emotions broaden and build. *Advances on Experimental Social Psychology, 47,* 1–53.

Gray, P. (2011). The decline of play and the rise of psychopathology in children and adolescents. *American Journal of Play, 3*(4), 443–463.

Grenville-Cleave, B. & Boniwell, I. (2012). Surviving or thriving? Do teachers have lower perceived control and well-being than other professions? *Management in Education, 26*(1), 3–5.

Hromek, R. & Roffey, S. (2009). Promoting social and emotional learning with games: "It's fun and we learn things". *Simulation & Gaming, 40*(5), 626–644.

Jenkins, L. (2019). *How to Create a Perfect School: Maintain Students' Motivation and Love of Learning from Kindergarten through 12th Grade.* LtOJ Press.

Johnston, O., Wildy, H. & Shand, J. (2023). Teenagers learn through play too: communicating high expectations through a playful learning approach. *The Australian Educational Researcher, 50,* 921–940.

Knoop, H., Holstein, B.E., Viskum, H. & Lindskov, J. (2016). *Fra kedsomhed til trivsel i skolen: Teori og data fra den nationale trivselsmaling.* DCUM. Cited in M. Ledertoug & N. Paarup, (2023). *The Quest for Optimal Learning.* Solve-it ApS.

New South Wales Commission for Children and Young People. (2002–2009). *Ask the Children.* Although the Commission and its website no longer exist, the National Library of Australia archived copies of the relevant pages, which can be accessed here: https://webarchive.nla.gov.au/tep/116783

Otake, K., Shimai, S., Tanaka-Matsumi, J., Otsui, K. & Fredrickson, B.L. (2006). Happy people become happier through kindness: A counting kindnesses intervention. *Journal of Happiness Studies, 7*(3), 361–375.

Petersen, C., Maier, S.F. & Seligman, M.E.P. (1995). *Learned Helplessness: A Theory for the Age of Personal Control.* Oxford University Press.

Petersen, C. & Seligman, M.E.P. (2004). *Character Strengths and Virtues: A Handbook of Classification*. OUP.

Proyer, R.T., Gander, F., Brauer, K. & Chick, G. (2021). Can playfulness be stimulated? A randomised placebo-controlled online playfulness intervention study on effects on trait playfulness, well-being, and depression. *Applied Psychology: Health and Well-Being, 13*(1), 129–151.

Roffey, S. (2011). *Changing Behaviour in Schools: Promoting Positive Relationships and Wellbeing*. Sage.

Seligman, M.E.P. (2006). *Learned Optimism: How to Change Your Mind and Your Life*. Vintage Books.

Sylvester, R. & Seldon, A. (Chairs) (2022). *Times Education Commission Report: Bringing Out the Best*. The Times.

Tidmund, L. (2021). Building positive emotions and playfulness. In M.L. Kern & M.L. Weymeher (Eds), *The Palgrave Handbook of Positive Education*. Palgrave Macmillan.

Other sources and further reading

Gill, T.R. (2007). *No Fear – Growing Up in a Risk Averse Society*. This is now out of print, but a full copy can be downloaded at: https://timrgill.files.wordpress.com/2010/10/no-fear-19-12-07.pdf

Hascher, T. & Waber, J. (2021). Teacher well-being: A systematic review of the research literature from the year 2000–2019. *Educational Research Review, 34*(2021), Article 100411.

Hattie, J. (2008). *Visible Learning: A Synthesis of over 800 Meta-Analyses Relating to Achievement*. Routledge.

Hattie, J. (2023). *Visible Learning: The Sequel. A Synthesis of over 2,100 Meta-Analyses Relating to Achievement*. Routledge.

Howells, K. (2012). *Gratitude in Education: A Radical View*. Sense Publishers.

McCallum, F. (2021). Teacher and staff wellbeing: Understanding the experiences of school staff. In M.L. Kern & M.L. Wehmeyer (Eds.), *The Palgrave Handbook of Positive Education* (open access). Palgrave Macmillan.

O'Brien, M. & Blue, L. (2018). Towards a positive pedagogy: designing pedagogical practices that facilitate positivity within the classroom. *Educational Action Research, 26*(3), 365–384.

Quinlan, D., Vella-Brodrick, D.A. Gray, A. & Swain, N. (2019). Teachers matter: Student outcomes following a strengths intervention are mediated by teacher strengths spotting. *Journal of Happiness Studies, 20*, 2507–2523.

Roffey, S. (Ed.) (2012a). *Positive Relationships: Evidence-Based Practice across the World*. Springer.

Roffey, S. (2012b). Pupil wellbeing: Teacher wellbeing: Two sides of the same coin? *Educational and Child Psychology, 29*(4), 817.

Roffey, S. (2017). Ordinary magic' needs ordinary magicians: The power and practice of positive relationships for building youth resilience and wellbeing. *Kognition und Paedagogik Social Resiliens, 103*, 38–57. Available in English at growinggreatschoolsworldwide.com/publications/articles

Roffey, S. (2019). *The Secondary Behaviour Cookbook: Strategies at Your Fingertips*. Routledge.

Singh, N. & Duraiappah, A.K. (2021). *Building Kinder Brains*. UNESCO MGIEP.

Resources

mgiep.unesco.org/article/kindness-the-force-that-will-help-us-achieve-sustainable-development-goals

mgiep.unesco.org/kindness

@teacher5aday – a twitter feed to support teacher wellbeing

Blog in *Education Week*: Carol Dweck revisits the growth mindset: edweek.org/leadership/opinion-carol-dweck-revisits-the-growth-mindset/2015/09

wellbeingstories.com/: These stories and the associated toolkits for teachers and families are written for upper primary aged children but may have relevance for Year 7 students. They put positive and negative thinking into characters. You can download the intro for free.

4 Inclusion

Everyone welcome, everyone matters, everyone participates

What do we mean by Inclusion?

Inclusion is a universal human right. It is seeing each individual as worthy of both respect and participation. It is not simply tolerating difference but accepting and celebrating each person's unique place in the world and also valuing our shared humanity – that we have more in common than divides us. It does not discriminate against anyone on account of their gender, race, sexuality, disability, religion, socio-economic status, ethnicity, idiosyncrasy or anything else. It challenges the definition of what is 'normal' and embraces the diversity that enriches us all. This chapter does not specify how to include different groups but details the principle of Inclusion and associated practices that apply to everyone, everywhere.

Although the continuums of inclusion/exclusion, school connectedness/rejection and belonging/alienation are discrete constructs, they are interdependent. For the purposes of this chapter, the first applies to actions taken at a school level, the second is what happens for individuals in a specific context, and the last is a feeling that can powerfully affect a student's perception of themselves and their attitudes to school, teachers, and learning.

Inclusive policies and practices are not just focused on those at risk of discrimination but the way all stakeholders in a school think about and treat each other. This is why you will find empathy in this chapter rather than in the one on Positivity (Chapter 3). Inclusion as a principle in positive education impacts on everyone, in both the learning environment and the future we are creating.

Belonging

We are hard-wired to connect with others. Babies do not smile at six weeks by accident: it enhances their chances of survival by positively engaging with – and rewarding – those who are caring for them. We all need to feel we belong somewhere. It is critical to our psychological and emotional wellbeing and is now known as one of the main factors for resilience and positive adaptation to adversity.

Most people feel they belong within their family – and in my experience, even students who have been badly treated by their parents will often still fiercely defend them. Other places where people might have a sense of belonging are in a school, sports club, faith group, friendship group, local gang, youth club, political party, neighbourhood, city or nation. There are also communities of shared interests and professions, some of which are online. Belonging is along a continuum – you are closer to some people than others, and it depends on context – what is happening at the time and how engaged you are with others. Cheering your team along with others on a Saturday afternoon can make you feel part of something highly significant!

There are, however, two aspects to belonging, and the difference is important.

DOI: 10.4324/9781003428244-5

Exclusive belonging

Exclusive belonging is where you are attached to a closed group. Being inside such a group can be protective and make you feel your presence matters, so can be positive for mental health, at least on the surface. It can provide reciprocal support and a sense of solidarity. But closed groups may be dominated by powerful individuals who establish and monitor the criteria for belonging. If you follow their rules, all may be well, but deviation can place you outside – either temporarily or for good.

Exclusive groups often maintain a sense of superiority over those who are outsiders and in some cases treat them as unworthy – even sub-human. Putnam (2000) refers to exclusive groups as demonstrating 'bonding' social capital, bound by "*a kind of sociological Super Glue*". Tight knit, inflexible, and maybe self-congratulatory, they can position other people outside the group as objects, having little concern or compassion for anyone not part of their community, an attitude he calls an 'I–it' orientation. This is most evident in strict religions or nationalistic governments. It was the basis of apartheid and the holocaust and is evident wherever politicians and/or the military stir up emotions against one group of people, facilitating cruelty and even genocide. You also find this exclusivity in online networks who reinforce each other's views, however damaging and erroneous these may be. People sometimes refer to these individuals as being in a 'bubble' where a certain sense of reality is shared, strengthened, and resists challenge, maybe demonising those who try. We need to teach students to be critical thinkers, so they are aware of how false information is spread and choose to make decisions about their lives on the evidence of what is real. Awareness of emotional manipulation and contagion may also help prevent exploitation and perhaps succumbing to peer pressure.

Leaving an exclusive group, especially if your identity is tied up with its norms and values, is a risk to stability, sense of self and support. It is only when something happens that deeply confronts a person's sense of who they are that they might consider this. Some individuals leave their families or exclusive communities to escape the restrictions imposed on them, perhaps over sexuality, authoritarian traditions or a conflict of values, but unless they are welcomed and accepted by others they may experience overwhelming loneliness and a challenge to their mental health and wellbeing.

Inclusive belonging

Inclusive belonging, on the other hand, is open to all. It values diversity and welcomes everyone. People do not quickly jump to judgment about individuals based on stereotypes and prejudice but instead show interest and seek understanding for an 'I–you' orientation where shared humanity is at the forefront of decisions. Putnam refers to this as 'bridging' social capital, the sociological equivalent of WD-40 – the lubricating substance used on metal machine parts to keep them moving and not getting stuck. An inclusive approach oils the wheels of relationships between groups, such as home and school. Inclusive belonging fosters healthy relationships and high social capital, making collaboration towards agreed goals more likely.

Some may see this as idealistic, but there is now a wealth of research (e.g. Philpot et al., 2020; Vlerick, 2021) that indicates that altruism and kindness towards others are part of the human condition and often enhance happiness and wellbeing for the giver as well as the receiver (Post, 2005). Empathy is reliably aroused in humans in response to misfortune in others but mediated by how we think about others and the situation they are in. We may not see much empathy in people with power at the macro level of an ecological framework, but there are always those who will stand up for others and intervene to protect them when and where they can.

Inclusion can, however, be challenging as it asks for privileged individuals and groups to relinquish some of what they have in order for distribution of resources to be fairer. This is likely to be resisted until people realise that, in the end, everyone benefits. We never know when we might need Inclusion to apply to us or the people we love.

Mattering

Isaac Prilleltensky has written extensively on 'mattering' (2020, 2021). He defines this as feeling valued but also being of value – making a recognised contribution. It is a feeling that you count, can make a difference, are trusted to do so, and that authentic opportunities are available. This is highly relatable across geographic and cultural boundaries.

Feeling valued begins in infancy with healthy attachment to primary carers. It then broadens out to a sense of belonging to a wider group – family, then community.

> *Dignity is the backbone of mattering … it is the quality of being worthy, honoured and esteemed. … It is the feeling of being recognised, acknowledged, included and respected for who we are or what we know … making us feel human.*
>
> (Prilleltensky & Prilleltensky, 2021, p. 32)

However, being valued is not enough to fully matter. To add value, we need to contribute. Adding value to enhance our lives personally can include learning, finding a passion or purpose, working towards a goal, or developing confidence in new competencies. Adding value to our communities can include emotional, physical, psychological, or practical support. It can be positive communication with others, helping, sharing, listening, being part of a team project, having a role in sporting or social events or volunteering. In schools all learners need opportunities to add value – this is aligned with the principle of Agency.

Belonging to school

What does it mean to belong to your school? In 1993, Goodenow and Grady defined this as "*the extent to which students feel personally accepted, respected, included, and supported by others in the school social environment*". It is also now acknowledged that school belonging is also aligned with purpose and progress in learning. Unless students can appreciate the relevance to their own lives of what is on the curriculum and perceive themselves as making progress, school as a hub of knowledge and understanding has little meaning for them.

The Wingspread Declaration on School Connections (2004) identified four factors that influence school connectedness. These are adult support, belonging to positive peer groups, commitment to education, and the quality of the school environment. Relationships are central. Students are more likely to feel they belong to school when they believe that the adults there are interested in them as people, care about their learning, and help them aim high. Teachers who try to make learning contextually relevant are also promoting a sense of belonging. Pupils disengage when learning is neither meaningful nor challenging, so it is unsurprising that researchers (Stevens et al., 2007) found that the more teachers encouraged ideas, supported goal setting and mastery, asked pupils to explain their work, and promoted learning over performance, the more students felt they belonged to their school.

Students also need to have friends they can rely on and with whom they feel safe. Those who are bullied by others because they are positioned as 'different' not only have a miserable time in school, but the impact of this behaviour can have long-lasting consequences for their mental health and wellbeing. All pupils need opportunities to discuss together and reflect on how they treat each other. This is one reason why social and emotional learning (SEL) needs to be at the core of education. There is more on addressing bullying in Chapter 2 on Safety.

Why does Inclusion matter?

Congruence with the United Nations Convention on the Rights of the Child

Article 2: Non-discrimination: The Convention applies to every child without discrimination, whatever their ethnicity, sex, religion, language, abilities or any other status, whatever they think or say, whatever their family background.

A sense of belonging to school has multiple benefits, including academic motivation and engagement, pro-social behaviour, reduced anxiety, stronger mental health and resilience, positive links with families and community and constructive peer relationships – reducing the incidence of bullying behaviours. Inclusive belonging in school also has implications for society beyond the immediate learning environment, potentially addressing racism, homophobia, misogyny and discrimination against minorities. Importantly, when young people feel alienated from school they will look for a sense of belonging elsewhere and are therefore potentially unsafe and vulnerable to exploitation.

Adolescent development

While a sense of belonging is important for pupils of all ages, it is particularly relevant for the needs and challenges of adolescence. The transition from childhood to adulthood includes not only major physical and sexual development but also significant cognitive and emotional changes. An important life-skill for teenagers is working out who they want to be, the values they hold, and what they believe. The support they seek during this stage of identify development is often with peers rather than adults. This is one reason why lockdown during Covid had a negative impact on adolescent mental health. Positive friendships and school belonging correlate with the formation of a positive identity, whereas negative experiences can have a profound effect on psychosocial adjustment (Allen et al., 2018).

School attendance and life trajectories

There is growing concern about increases in exclusions, alienation, and a sense of 'not belonging' in school and the impact of this on young people's well-being and life chances. In the UK, research indicates that 1 in 4 pupils do not feel they belong in school (Riley et al., 2020), and this number increases with those from more disadvantaged communities, black pupils, and those identified as having special educational needs. Black students are excluded in the UK four times as often as others, and a similar picture is evident with Aboriginal students – especially boys – in Australia. This is mirrored in statistics about later incarceration; 25 times more indigenous youth than non-indigenous youth are sent to prison. Excluding students from school may give short-term relief to teachers, but it has considerable implications for the life trajectory of those who miss out.

The impact of the Covid-19 pandemic on school attendance has been widely reported. There are estimates that the number of students in the UK who are more out of school than in has increased by 108%, with 1 in 5 regularly absent. Those most at risk are those in secondary school whose families are struggling with debt or homelessness, pupils with health issues or are carers for family members, and those with additional needs. High levels of anxiety also contribute, as do practices such as informally 'off-rolling' young people who present with difficulties and/or lower a school's academic results.

The concern is not just about students missing education but also their invisibility and whether anyone is monitoring their safety. We hear grim stories about some 'falling through the net' and experiencing abuse and exploitation.

Forcing students to go to school or punishing their parents for non-compliance undermines the supportive relationships that foster belonging and motivate pupils to want to be there.

In *Square Pegs* (Morgan & Costello, 2023), we read about many children and young people who are simply unable to go to school. They don't fit in. This has been traditionally considered a problem within the student – something is wrong with them. Alternatively, they are labelled as being non-compliant and potentially delinquent 'truants'. The push/pull analysis, once a popular conceptual framework for non-attendance, is now seen as limited. The pull factors are things going on at home or in the community, such as bereavement, family violence or mental health concerns that are perceived as more important than school. The push factors are what is happening at school that makes pupils not want to be there, such as bullying, intimidation, or constant pressure to perform. Environmental and social issues have had less attention but are also powerful. This includes poverty, transport, political policies, school priorities and access to support, especially for those with special educational needs and disability. Schools that are inflexible with a 'one size fits all' approach are unable to cater for these pupils. When square pegs do not fit in round holes, we need to make square holes.

The organisation 'Not Fine in School' was set up to provide a resource and support to families where pupils experience attendance problems and barriers. At the time of writing the Facebook group has nearly 43,000 followers. Dr Beth Bodycote interviewed members of this organisation on the problems and barriers to school attendance they had encountered and what helped. This is a brief summary of what helps:

- A resolution is more likely to be achieved when a pupil has early access to help.
- Parental concerns are too often dismissed and need to be taken seriously.
- It is valuable to work towards a shared understanding of difficulties.
- Authorising absence for both physical or mental health issues and giving support where possible relieve the fear of blame and possible legal action.
- Teachers who respect parental knowledge of their child, acknowledge their own limitations, show empathy, and have a focus on the young person's wellbeing contribute to a positive working relationship with families.
- Parents are often in genuine need of advice and systemic support, not dismissal, judgment or condemnation.
- Young people are empowered by having some control of the situation, so they have the flexibility to make small steps of progress with minimal pressure.
- Helping students stay in touch with others may support a successful return.
- Measures need to be put in place to effectively address bullying.
- Providing schoolwork to do at home relieves the pressure of 'catching up.'
- Regular, reliable and positive communication between home and school helps maintain positive relationships.
- Prompt referral to services and for assessment.
- Local authorities need to be consistent in complying with legislation for 'education other than at school' and special needs and disability (SEND).
- Patience – these issues are complex and resolution takes time – and sometimes experimentation.

The pressures on students and families often become untenable with escalating levels of stress. This negatively affects relationships, mental health, family functioning and even finances when someone has to be at home. Things only improve when parents accept the situation and begin to prioritise their child's wellbeing above compliance with authorities and cultural expectations. Mainstream school is not for everyone, and academic success is not the only way to a life well lived.

Feelings of rejection

In Chapter 3 on Positivity we talk about the importance of positive feelings in the classroom and how these promote cognitive skills and pro-social behaviours. This is even more important when we consider the implications of negative feelings.

Exclusion and rejection are powerful instigators of emotions that can have far-reaching consequences. Social rejection activates many of the same brain regions involved in physical pain, and it is now acknowledged that the pain of being excluded is on a par with that of physical hurt. Social rejection can influence not only mental health but also cognition and even physical health. It may also have wider and more dangerous implications, leading to aggression and even violence. In 2003, Leary and colleagues analysed 15 cases of school shooters and found all but two suffered from social rejection.

Teen killers don't come from schools that foster a sense of belonging

This headline in the *New Scientist* reported on research by Wike and Fraser (2009), who summarized their findings in an academic article entitled *School Shootings: Making sense of the senseless*. They explored patterns across multiple incidents to enable understanding of both the individual factors motivating shooting events and the characteristics of schools where shootings have occurred.

"Shootings appear more likely in schools characterized by a high degree of social stratification, low bonding and attachment between teachers and students, and few opportunities for involvement. High risk school cultures are unresponsive to the needs of students, provide rewards and recognition for only an elite few, and create social dynamics that promote disrespectful behaviour, bullying, and peer harassment."

Their recommendations to prevent such incidents are:
Strengthening school attachment

- reducing social aggression
- breaking down codes of silence
- establishing screening and intervention protocols for troubled and rejected students
- bolstering human and physical security
- increasing communication within educational facilities and between educational facilities and local resources.

Wider implications of belonging

When someone is included by a group and feels that they belong there, they are more likely to see this community as important to them, cooperate with others and abide by the behaviours expected to stay connected. This has much wider implications than at first appears.

People do things on the basis of belief and what they feel. This is not religious belief, but what makes sense to them about the way the world works. We tend to believe a 'reality' that fits with the dominant culture – or at least the one we feel an attachment to. If the rhetoric engages emotions that promote a sense of belonging and purpose, this can build motivation to engage with a shared endeavour. Young men and women have historically signed up to fulfil their 'patriotic duty' by going to war. Those who did not do this were often ostracised by others in the community. Although it may be uncomfortable to consider, there are parallels with those who are persuaded to commit acts of terrorism. When young people are told that they will achieve 'glory' if they attack those who represent 'Western' values and practices, and there are few other avenues open to their feeling important, then fighting for such a cause may be appealing.

As acts of terrorism are often perpetrated by 'home-grown' terrorists, many of whom have been educated in the country in which these acts take place, schools might reduce the risk by promoting a culture of inclusive belonging (Boyle & Roffey, 2018).

There is a similar argument for gang membership. Ngo et al. (2015) examined criminal gang involvement of immigrant youth in Canada and found that over time they had experienced disintegration of their relationships with family, school and community. This had negatively impacted on their self-concept, ethnic identity, sense of belonging and sense of citizenship. The National Youth Agency in the UK (2020) also point to the recruitment of young people from more 'vulnerable' family backgrounds into street and criminal gangs, an issue that has accelerated since Covid-19, when services and support have been less available, including from schools. Finding ways to motivate teenagers to be in school and feel they have purpose and a sense of belonging there is more critical than ever.

Resilience and mental health

Resilience is the ability to cope with and thrive in the face of one or more negative life events, whereas positive adaptation refers to how someone might respond to chronic adverse experiences in ways that enhance a positive sense of self and healthy relationships. The latter is, of course, much harder to achieve. Research has shown that there are both personal and environmental factors that increase the chances of doing well despite severe challenges and that one of these factors is feeling you belong. The others are having someone who believes in the best of you and has high expectations of what you might do and who you might become (Werner and Smith, 2001). All these are encapsulated in high-quality teacher–student relationships. Teachers can make more difference than they realise, and policymakers need to acknowledge how much this matters to both wellbeing and learning.

Behaviour

When young people feel respected as part of the school community, they are much more likely to want to stay connected – and their behaviour will often reflect this. They may still have triggering moments when they are out of control, but will be more remorseful afterwards and willing, if not eager, to 'restore' their connection. See *Behaviour & restorative practice* in this chapter.

Inclusion in practice in the secondary classroom

It is the relationships that pupils have with teachers and peers that most strongly mediate feelings of belonging. It is not just sharing the same space that matters but whether or not these relationships are warm, accepting, supportive and fair. Micro-moments matter.

The words that are said as well as simple actions can be momentary, but when they happen on a regular basis they provide the foundation for pupils to feel that their presence is welcomed and valued. The way that teachers interact with students – and also with each other – provides a model for how students should interact with others.

Teacher–student relationships

The quality of teacher–student relationships often declines in secondary school along with school belonging, but with the numbers of young people disengaging with learning this might be considered a priority for development.

School belonging is enhanced for those students who believe that the adults in the school care about their learning, are interested in them as individuals, and maintain high expectations of them. Both Hattie (2008) and Allen et al. (2018) in their meta-analyses found a large effect for the quality of teacher–student relationships: Hattie specifically in enhancing academic outcomes, and Allen et al. between teacher support and school belonging. Student perceptions of how much a teacher cares appear to be influenced by whether both curriculum content and pedagogy resonate with them. The more that teachers promote learning over performance, the more belonging students experience.

A good rapport, including with students who are not high achievers, is enhanced when teachers show that they respect and value students, show interest in them as people, and provide guidance and emotional support where needed.

A simple intervention that involved teachers and students finding out five commonalities they shared reduced the achievement gap in one school by an astonishing 60% (Gehlbach et al., 2016). This is easily replicable in schools, and clearly worth doing.

Simply greeting students by name in the morning and smiling, looking pleased to see them, can significantly increase a sense of belonging. Seeing every day as a new day and not being judgmental or bearing grudges also help.

What students say about belonging

367 Australian secondary students were asked to say what factors influenced their sense of belonging in school (Allen et al., 2021). Analysis revealed that teachers could make a difference in four ways: emotional support, support for learning, social support and respect for diversity. School-level practices included school-wide social and emotional support, activities and opportunities for social connection, respect, equity and diversity, positive school culture, supportive and effective teachers, environment and safety, and student voice and choice. Student voices from the open-ended aspect of the survey powerfully illustrate these themes:

"Don't yell at the student if they get an answer wrong, we are trying to learn what you are teaching us but … this is one of the most confusing times in our lives and we are trying to discover who we are at the same time."

"not pick favourites, treat everyone equally."

"more LGBTQIA+ inclusivity and teachers taking notice of any hateful language being said, because it needs to be taken more seriously."

"[create a] rich community of students where students who don't know each other can easily have a conversation".

There was also appreciation for what schools are already doing:

"My school has extra-curricular activities I can join."
"My school has activities at break times where I can go if I don't want to sit with someone."
"My school teaches skills that help me make and keep friends."

Kelly-Ann Allen, Associate Professor Monash University

Teaching and learning

Supportive teachers consider different learning levels and keep students' views in mind when conducting and scaffolding activities in the classroom. This enables pupils to engage more fully with learning and perceive themselves as making progress. Positive psychologist Mihalyi Csikszentmihalyi (2002) writes about the concept of 'flow' as the moment in which individuals are at their happiest and most engaged. In schools this would equate to where a pupil has enough prior learning to tune into the subject, so they see any challenge presented as building on their knowledge base and therefore achievable. This aligns with intrinsic motivation. Where something is entirely outside a pupil's frame of reference, they may be confused, anxious and possibly switched off. If the material presented is too easy or overly repetitive then there is a risk of boredom. Another educational pioneer, Vygotsky (1978), talked about learning happening in 'the zone of proximal development', which is a similar conceptual framework to 'flow'.

Meeting the needs of diverse learners in a class is clearly a highly demanding task for teachers when they are expected to deliver the same curriculum content regardless. There are, however, recommendations on ways to maximise engagement with learning – most educators will already be familiar with these:

1   Reducing distractions from the learning experience itself, such as tests and rules
2   Identifying, acknowledging, and fostering pupil interests and strengths
3   Clarifying the goals of the task so pupils know what they are aiming for. For some pupils this means breaking down a task into smaller steps so that they are not overwhelmed and see the task as achievable.
4   Providing specific feedback on what has been achieved and the next step
5   Encouraging self-evaluation: *"What was good about that piece of work?"*, *"What could you do better?"*, and *"What help do you need?"*
6   Asking students to give feedback to teachers on what sense they have made of the task.

The use of 'personal bests' has potential in the classroom, as pupils competing against themselves cannot be losers! It reduces competition with others and enables pupils to take pride in their own achievements.

Co-operative and project-based learning enables pupils to learn from each other and be stimulated by new ideas. Vygotsky emphasised the value of social interactions in learning and the potential of peer support.

Peer relationships

Although teacher–student relationships have received most attention in the literature, it is relationships with peers that invariably make the most difference to a sense of belonging and inclusion. Although much of this has focused on negative interactions such as bullying, a number of researchers have found that the positive social aspect of school – meeting friends there – is a powerful motivator for school attendance (Gorard & See, 2011; Gowing, 2019)

Great to see all my mates again after five days. Everyone was so happy and had loads of stories to share. Makes you feel good when your friends laugh and joke with you. I look forward to school because of my mates, because they make me feel so alive. (Senior Male).

(from Gowing, 2019)

Beyond companionship and the simple enjoyment of socialising, friends in high school are also a key source of support when things are tough. It is not surprising that the disconnection emanating from the pandemic had far-reaching implications for both attendance and mental health. Strategies for connecting and re-connecting young people are critical within the learning environment.

Regularly mixing students up, so that they work with everyone else in the class and get to know them, can help develop knowledge and understanding of each other. This is a more effective strategy for inclusion and belonging than ability or friendship groups.

Young people need regular opportunities to interact with each other in a safe, solution-focused environment. SEL has been downgraded in some countries but is increasingly recognised by significant bodies such as the OECD and UNESCO as critical for young people to become more connected, share positive strategies for coping, and reduce prejudice and discrimination. Further strategies for doing this are in the SEL section at the end of this chapter.

Empathy

Including others requires empathy – being able to tune into others and their needs. When individuals grow up in warm, supportive and inclusive families, they often learn to do this from an early age, but that is not the case for every student. Some need to discover what empathy means, by both experiencing it and having opportunities to learn and develop it. Empathy has several manifestations, but it includes being able to tune into the emotional context and appreciate what others are feeling. It begins by reflecting on "what would this situation be like if it was happening to me – so how might it be for others?" This can be embedded in many aspects of the curriculum, such as reviewing events in history and scientific achievements that made a difference to many lives, exploring the conflicting emotions of characters in novels, or sharing stories of those who are experiencing the impact of the climate crisis. Empathy in practice also means not jumping to conclusions about the motivations or intentions of others but being able to think critically before making judgments, seeking evidence rather than depending on anecdotes or scare stories on social media.

Inclusion in practice across the secondary school

Although individual teachers can do a lot to support a sense of belonging with the young people they interact with on a regular basis, this will not be sustainable across years unless Inclusion is prioritised across the whole school. There is no blueprint, as each school is operating within a different context, and senior leadership teams will need to liaise with stakeholders to establish the most effective ways of doing this.

A meta-analysis of 51 studies (Allen et al., 2018) identified many individual- and social-level factors that influence school belonging. These core themes include academic factors, personal characteristics, social relationships, demographic characteristics, school climate and extra-curricular activities. For many of the determinants of school belonging, University College, the Institute of Education and the National Teachers Union (Riley et al., 2020) researched place and belonging in school and identified three interconnected themes that underpinned intentional positive school practice:

- Leadership creates culture.
- Culture shapes learning and behaviour.
- Together these shape agency and belonging.

Transition to secondary from primary

Transitions are often hard, because they entail loss as well as potentially positive changes. Moving into a new school can be scary. It is not only differences in academic expectations that students may find challenging but also the social aspects of secondary school – making new friends, being safe from bullying, feeling you belong (Keay et al., 2015). Schools can do much to alleviate anxiety and promote positive interactions (Baharara, 2020). Several activities are described in the SEL section of this chapter, but the following also help:

- Asking students to work together to devise guidelines for a safe and inclusive class rather than imposing a set of rules
- Regularly mixing students up so that they work and interact with a variety of peers
- Giving students opportunities to have safe but structured conversations with each other and perhaps introducing scripts to support this such as follow-up questions to show interest. Getting to know each other reduces stereotyping and prejudice
- Offering a range of activities in unstructured times of the day so that students can both develop interests and meet others who share them
- Encouraging involvement with school activities such as sport, community action, and music. This gives opportunities to be of value as well as valued.

Connecting communities

We live in challenging times with many communities, most of whom want to live in peace and harmony, are torn apart by the actions of a minority and the rhetoric that accompanies this. As history tells us, unless nations are obliterated by inhumane practices, the only answer to peace is through conversation and negotiation where there is a genuine desire to understand the other and perhaps walk in their shoes. Seeking our shared humanity has better options than focusing on what divides us. What happens in education has far-reaching consequences for the future of our world. How can we promote a sense of inclusion in schools where there are major cultural differences and often an entrenched cultural racism? The following case studies give us both food for thought and a spark of optimism.

Together for Humanity

Together for Humanity (TFH) is an organisation based in Australia that works across school communities to foster intercultural understanding and help students learn how to deal with differences. Their programs are delivered by mixed teams of facilitators from diverse backgrounds in terms of religious beliefs and cultures. Two of the factors that are key to TFH programs are empathy and inter-group contact. Teachers also need to model positive interactions between each other so that they are part of the whole process.

An effective method for invoking empathy is hearing the stories of others and their lived experience. Calisha Bennett, a facilitator of TFH programs, tells students about her experience at school as a Muslim girl wearing a Hijab:

> *On my first day at a public high school in a regional town in Western Australia, a large hoard of curious students followed along behind me as I was given a tour of the school … I would secretly fast during Ramadan, explaining for days on end to my friends that I simply 'wasn't hungry' during recess and lunch. Lord knows they probably thought I had an eating disorder!*

For many students Calisha is the first Muslim they ever met. In some programs students from different schools and cultural and religious backgrounds spend a few days together, participating in fun learning activities and discussion.

One participant in a TFH interschool program reflected on her experience:

> *Many [Muslim] girls were saying, 'We are going into a Jewish school, what would happen, would we get attacked?' We walked in and nothing happened… our mindset completely changed…we've seen how different people are like us … It's opened my mind to different cultures, putting myself in different shoes".*

(Gale et al., 2019)

A qualitative evaluation of this intervention (Gale et al., 2019) indicated that TFH programs were effective in assisting students to challenge stereotypes and alleviate their fears.

> *They enabled respectful, sometimes tough, conversations within constructed spaces of equality and reciprocity and promoted the acquisition of empathy and mutual acceptance and belonging. Students gained skills and confidence [that went beyond] just interacting with people with different cultural backgrounds … In all this, they discovered within cultural difference their common humanity and interdependence.*

One student told the evaluators:

> *I used to be a massive prejudice, but now [I know] I can't judge a whole community based off one guy's actions. … it's really helped me out.*

Rabbi Zalman Kastel, dean and founder, Together for Humanity

We do not seek evidence in order to form our beliefs; we seek evidence that will support our existing beliefs. People want their beliefs to be 'reasonable', so when they are directly challenged by 'evidence' a likely response is to give reasons that strongly defend them. Listening respectfully to why people hold the views they do and having conversations that focus on what is reasonable rather than trying to undermine beliefs are often more effective in encouraging reflection. People change their minds when both their experiences and the conversations around them make it impossible to maintain both existing beliefs together with an appreciation of themselves as reasonable. We see this in the changing views on climate and also in what we believe about others.

Still hoping and working for peace

Israel is a highly diverse country with separate education systems. In most cases, higher education institutions are the first opportunity for Arab and Jewish students to meet. Learning together may present an opportunity for communicating, interacting, and engaging with 'others'. If there is no concern, however, for improving intergroup relations in mixed academic institutions, when the reality outside is divided and conflictual, intergroup interaction can provoke tensions and conflicts.

As an institution we take many actions to create a safe place for everyone and encourage diversity on faculty and student boards. We take students through a process of selecting together the guiding values that they want to live by as a group. Faculty are trained on how to work with diverse groups, and wide support is provided to those for whom Hebrew is not their first language.

My work in cultivating social-emotional competencies with students provides an opportunity for improving intergroup relationships, one which is relevant also for secondary students and even younger. Discussing emotions, thoughts and social-emotional competencies allows students to share and listen to others share their emotional experiences, bringing them closer, seeing others as unique individuals, finding communalities, and developing empathy. For example, right after a terror attack, an Arab student described how scared he is to walk on the streets and serve clients at a coffee shop he works in. This was eye-opening to Jewish students who themselves were scared. When all students are heard, they feel a sense of inclusion and belonging. Learning takes place through working in pairs, small groups and sharing in a whole-class form, experimenting with emotion games or designing activities for the class in mixed groups. As part of their assignments, students then go back to their hometowns and deliver lessons to children and youth. Recently, we involved pairs of students – Jewish and Arab – in working with diverse groups, which was found to create strong bonds between the students.

Dr Niva Dolev, Education and Community Department and Dean of Students, Kinneret College in the Sea of Galilee

(This was written during the first days of the Israel–Hamas war – it might feel like a drop of hope in the ocean of hate, but unless we work with our young people to build understanding and connection, nothing will ever change for the better – my deep thanks to Niva for her work – SR.)

Community and home relationships

Notices, directions and labels across a school need to be in the languages of those communities that the school serves. Posters on the walls that reflect achievements of people who look like the pupils in the school are more likely to motivate them.

The relationship between school and home is a two-way street, but the initiative to promote inclusion begins with the school. Asking for involvement in an open and general way is less likely to help families feel connected than if schools request specific support that values their culture. This could include:

• Asking for advice about cultural celebrations and involving community groups in leading school activities

- Invitations to write for a school's newsletter or speak to students, perhaps on aspects of lived experience
- Putting out requests for practical help when appropriate, such as teams to develop a school garden
- Ensuring that communities are represented on governing bodies and parent groups.

The school being visible in the community also helps, such as being present at local festivities. Continually reviewing community relations is vital as groups move on to be replaced by different individuals.

World Café

World Café is a way of sharing knowledge, generating ideas, and constructing dialogues with groups. Although more commonly used with students, this is a way of involving parents and community in the life of the school and getting their views on specific issues. It provides an opportunity to matter by contributing to discussion and being of value.

Participants are sent an invitation which gives options for days and times. Several World Cafés may be offered, to include as many families and communities as possible. It may be necessary to translate invitations and engage translators.

Families are welcomed by the facilitator, who explains the process and encourages the discussion to be positive, solution-focused and respectful to all – even when disagreeing. Parents sit four or five to a table and discuss the question(s) they have been given. For example:

- What helps students feel they belong to school?
- What helps families feel connected to this school?
- What else would help?

One person at the table keeps a note of what is said. You can choose to have a different question on each table. After 20 minutes everyone except the scribe gets up and changes tables. The idea is to mix everyone up to talk with new people. The scribe quickly summarises what was said by the first group, and then the second discussion begins.

After another 20 minutes there is another change, with the scribe taking the same role.

At the end of the hour the facilitator summarises the discussion and thanks the families for their participation. Decisions taken by the school on the basis of these discussions are communicated to parents/communities.

Behaviour & restorative practice

Zero-tolerance behaviour policies do not work over the longer term and lead to a 'school to prison pipeline'. The American Psychological Association published the research from their Zero-Tolerance Task Force (2008), which found that not only did behaviour not improve across the school, it worsened outcomes in learning, as there were always others to replace the students excluded. Relationships became authoritarian rather than supportive. Their recommendations include a whole-community approach and restorative practices.

Restorative practice emphasises communication, empathy, and accountability. Rather than focusing on sanctions that often exclude a student from their peers, it emphasises reconciliation and reintegration. It positions unacceptable behaviour as harm to the community and looks to resolve conflict and repair this harm. As practitioner Bill Hansberry says:

> *As communities become increasingly disconnected and fearful of one another, responses to conflict, harm and wrongdoing that bring people and their difficult emotions face to face can seem too risky, yet schools who have bravely embraced restorative practices have found that this is a risk well worth taking.*

It takes time and training to establish effective restorative practice, requiring everyone in the school to understand what it entails, be supportive of the approach, and ensure that other policies and practices are compatible. It does not simply consist of a set of statements and questions. It begins with creating community but once established is far more effective over the longer term as it changes not just behaviour from the inside out but relationships and responsibility. The aim is to maintain a sense of community by:

- Providing pathways to repair the harm done
- Bringing together everyone who has been affected in a dialogue that works towards achieving a common understanding
- Coming to an agreement about resolving the conflict and moving forward.

Restorative approaches can be seen as part of a broader ethos or culture that identifies strong, mutually respectful relationships and a cohesive community as the foundations on which good teaching and learning can flourish.

School uniform

The issue of uniform in school is controversial and advocates for either having or not having one are often strongly committed to their position. Like many things, it is not just what pupils wear that matters but what it represents, and how uniform policy is implemented. Wearing the same outfit as others might indicate the school a pupil attends but does not promote a sense of belonging unless that individual is already proud and pleased to be associated with the school. For those who feel alienated it can be something to either tolerate or resist. A focus on uniform infringements is a major problem. When pupils are singled out or given sanctions for having the 'wrong' shoes, a poorly knotted tie, or an 'unacceptable' hairstyle, this can undermine positive relationships and a sense of belonging. The more specific and detailed the uniform requirements are, the more expensive for parents and the more opportunities for critical conversations. Alternatives to that could include students wearing jeans of their choice and a T-shirt with the school's name or a recommendation for a simple colour code – such as everyone wearing red and grey. Trousers for all reduces the safety concerns posed by skirt length.

Teacher belonging

Research by the National Education Union on belonging and agency (Riley et al., 2020) found that teachers' sense of belonging was vital in not only promoting a positive whole-school culture that enhanced connectedness but also teacher retention. Teachers in this survey talked about the difference this made to them:

- *"You can be more creative, innovative, and confident."*
- *"You feel respected and accepted."*

- *"You'll stay longer in an organisation and make more of a contribution."*
- *"You have a sense of well-being and agency."*
- *"You feel more involved and committed to your job."*

One teacher summed it up as follows: *"you commit and know you have a future and that encourages you to be yourself and to innovate."*

Inclusion in social and emotional learning (SEL)

The Inclusion principle in Circle Solutions is activated by regularly mixing students up so that they talk with those outside their usual social circle. Doing this in a variety of games makes it less likely that pupils gravitate only to close friends. As Circles continue over time, getting to know others they wouldn't normally talk to becomes something that students look forward to and enjoy. This in itself promotes connection and inhibits prejudice and stereotyping. As teachers are full participants in Circle Solutions, they also find out more about their pupils in these activities, fostering positive relationships and understanding.

Activities in SEL

These not only explore how we think about others but also aim to promote interest and understanding the values of good relationships. It is important that the teacher is aware of the context of their class so that they do not inadvertently raise issues that are especially difficult for some.

Pair shares

Finding what partners have in common – everyone having the same conversation. This can include facts about their lives, what they like or don't like, and what they think about an issue. For example:

- What they both like/hate to eat
- Sports they both enjoy – either playing or watching
- A funny cartoon/film/programme they have both seen
- What cheers them both up when they are feeling down
- Someone they both admire and look up to and why.

The teacher can then go round the Circle – perhaps using a talking stick to indicate whose turn it is – with the pairs beginning a sentence "We both ..."
   It is fine for pairs to repeat what others have said – this again shows commonalities.

Paired interviews

This is each partner finding out about the other. It is the basis of good conversations – showing interest, asking good questions, listening to the answers, and taking turns to speak. Topics given by the teacher can be expanded but might include the following:

- Family celebrations
- Random act of kindness

– Favourite book
– A long journey
– A big celebration in the future
– What super-power would you like to have and why

There are hundreds of topics to choose from but also many useful resources to help busy teachers.

Small group/whole-class activities

Strengths in Circles Cards

There are seven statements for each of the six ASPIRE principles.
  These are four of those for Inclusion:

* We challenge stereotypes.
* We accept each other.
* We have goodwill towards each other.
* We believe everyone has something to offer.

In groups of three or four, students take one statement at a time and discuss the following questions together.

– What does this mean? What would we see and hear?
– Is this what we want in our school?
– What would it make people feel about being here?
– Is it already happening – how do we know?
– What else might we do?

Each group decides on one action. They give a brief report back to the Circle, emphasising the action. What they all agree on is put on display as a reminder.

Hypothetical

A student volunteers to read out a brief story about a fictional pupil in a particular situation. This is one about including a pupil who has experienced racism:

My name is Adebayo. I am quite good at football and play for my school. I am African, my family are from Nigeria. Sometimes at away matches, I get racist comments. It is horrible, and I don't know what to do about it. I am thinking about leaving the team. No-one seems to notice.

The pupils work in groups of three or four. They are asked these questions one at a time:

– How would you feel if you were Ade?
– Is this behaviour acceptable? Give reasons.

– Can Ade sort this on his own?
– What could this group do to help?
– What actions will make this happen?

The last is important as it puts theory into action – this is often left out so that actual practice does not change. This not only gives students agency, it also addresses what might need to happen at a whole-school level.

Not jumping to judgment

Small groups of three or four pupils are given an envelope with a picture on the front of something that might belong to a young person. This might be an item for sport or a hobby, a pet, or something to wear. The group spends a couple of minutes talking about the item and what this might tell them about the person who owns it. In the envelope are three statements that say more about the person. For example:

– *She is a refugee.*
– *He helps his father every Saturday at their market stall.*
– *They are the youngest of seven children and live with their grandmother.*
– *She loves music.*
– *They were in an accident and now don't see well.*

The group takes out one at a time and then discusses how this statement might make them see the person differently.
   At the end of the activity the groups are asked to talk about what they learnt by doing this activity and what difference it might make to how they see people in the future.

Inclusion checklist

INCLUSION	This is in place – we know it is effective because …	Working on it – our actions to date are …	Just started – our next step will be …
Welcome and support in place for new pupils			
Asking students what helps them feel they belong			
Asking students what helps them to learn			
Notices/directions in community languages			
School celebrates community festivals			
SEL activities to value diversity and promote inclusion			
Restorative approaches to behaviour			
Time protected for teachers to get to know students			
Friendship/inclusion activities that inhibit bullying behaviours			
Flexible responses for students who are struggling with attendance			

Inclusion in the future

If we are going to build a healthier, safer, and more cohesive society, we need to ensure that young people feel they belong to school and see themselves thriving there. We need to teach and model the value of diversity and our shared humanity. This includes honouring the unique value of every student, whatever their ability, background or aspiration, as well as acknowledging our commonalities.

Engaging fully with families and community also builds the positive connections that impact on student wellbeing and learning. Community Schools make both economic and educational sense. This is not just a school run by a local authority, but where it becomes the hub of a community, open to all and providing services and support that fit each neighbourhood's needs. It is created and run by the people who live there together with school staff. Although Community Schools are not yet a feature of the UK educational landscape they are being established elsewhere, such as in the US, where research indicates they have much to offer (Maier et al., 2017).

References, further reading and resources

Allen, K.-A., Kern, M.L., Vella-Brodrick, D.A., Hattie, J. & Waters, L. (2018). What schools need to know about fostering school belonging: A meta-analysis. *Educational Psychology Review*, *30*(1), 1–34.

Allen, K.-A., Slaten, C.D., Arslan, G., Roffey, S., Craig, H. & Vella-Brodrick, D.A. (2021). School belonging: The importance of student and teacher relationships. In M.L. Kern & M.L. Wehmeyer (Eds.), *The Palgrave Handbook of Positive Education*. Palgrave Macmillan.

American Psychological Association Zero Tolerance Task Force. (2008). Are zero tolerance policies effective in the schools?: An evidentiary review and recommendations. *American Psychologist*, *63*(9), 852–862.

Bharara, G. (2020). Factors facilitating a positive transition to secondary school: A systematic literature review. *International Journal of School & Educational Psychology*, *8*(1), 104–123.

Bodycote, B. (2023). School attendance problems and barriers. In F. Morgan & E. Costello (Eds.), *Square Pegs* (pp. 35–56). Independent Thinking Press.

Boyle, C. & Roffey, S. (2018). Belief, belonging and the role of schools in reducing the risk of home-grown extremism. In K.-A. Allen & C. Boyle (Eds.), *Pathways to School Belonging*. Brill Sense.

Csikszentmihalyi, M. (2002). *Flow: The Classic Work on How to Achieve Happiness*. Rider.

Gale, F., Edenborough, M., Boccanfuso E., Hawkins, M. & Sell, C. (2019). *Promoting Intercultural Understanding, Connectedness and Belonging: An Independent Qualitative Evaluation of Together for Humanity Programs*. Western Sydney University.

Gehlbach, H., Brinkworth, M.E., Hsu, L., King, A., McIntyre, J. & Rogers, T. (2016). Creating birds of similar feathers: Leveraging similarity to improve teacher-student relationships and academic achievement. *Journal of Educational Psychology*, *108*(3).

Goodenow, C. & Grady, K.E. (1993). The relationship of school belonging and friends' values to academic motivation among urban adolescent students. *The Journal of Experimental Education*, *62*(1), 60–71.

Gorard, S. & See, B.H. (2011). How can we enhance enjoyment of secondary school? The student view. *British Educational Research Journal*, *37*(4), 671–690.

Gowing, A. (2019). Peer-peer relationships: A key factor in enhancing school connectedness and belonging. *Educational and Child Psychology*, *36*(2), 64–77.

Hattie, J. (2008). *Visible Learning: A Synthesis of Over 800 Meta-Analyses Relating to Achievement*. Routledge.

Kastel, Z. (2012). Positive relations between members of groups with divergent beliefs and cultures. In S. Roffey (Ed.) *Positive Relationships: Evidence-Based Practice Across the World*. Springer.

Keay, A., Lang, J. & Frederickson, N. (2015). Comprehensive support for peer relationships at secondary transition. *Educational Psychology in Practice*, 31(3), 79–292.

Leary, M.R., Kowalski, R.M., Smith, L. & Phillips, S. (2003). Teasing, rejection, and violence: Case studies of the school shootings. *Aggressive Behavior*, 29(3), 202–214.

Maier, A., Daniel, J., Oakes, J. & Lam, L. (2017). *Community Schools as an Effective School Improvement Strategy: A Review of the Evidence*. Learning Policy Institute.

Morgan, F. & Costello, E. (2023). *Square Pegs: Inclusivity, Compassion and Fitting In. A Guide for Schools*. Independent Thinking Press.

National Youth Agency (2020). '*Hidden in plain sight*' – *A youth work response to gangs and exploitation during COVID-19*. nya.org.uk/hidden-in-plain-sight

Ngo, H., Calhoun, A., Worthington, C., Pyrch, T., & Este, D. (2015). The unravelling of identities and belonging: Criminal gang involvement of youth from immigrant families. *Journal of International Migration and Integration*, 18. doi: 10.1007/s12134-015-0466-5

Philpot, R., Liebst, L.S., Levine, M., Bernasco, W. & Lindegaard, M.R. (2020). Would I be helped? Cross-national CCTV footage shows that intervention is the norm in public conflicts. *American Psychologist*, 75(1), 66–75.

Post, S. (2005). Altruism, happiness, and health: It's good to be good. *International Journal of Behavioral Medicine*, 12(2), 66–77.

Prilleltensky, I. (2020). Mattering at the intersection of psychology, philosophy and politics. *Am. J. Community Psychol.*, 65, 16–34.

Prilleltensky, I. & Prilleltensky, O. (2021). *How People Matter: Why it Affects Health, Happiness, Love, Work and Society*. Cambridge University Press.

Putnam, R.D. (2000). *Bowling Alone: The Collapse and Revival of American Community*. Simon & Schuster.

Riley, K., Coates, M. & Allen, T. (2020). *Place and Belonging in School: Why it Matters Today*. Case-studies Art of Possibilities, UCL, Institute of Education, NTEU.

Stevens, T., Hamman, D. & Olivárez, A., Jr. (2007). Hispanic students' perception of white teachers' mastery goal orientation influences sense of school belonging. *Journal of Latinos and Education*, 6(1), 55–70.

Vlerick, M. (2021). Explaining human altruism. *Synthese*, 199, 2395–2413.

Vygotsky, L.S. (1978). *Mind and Society: The Development of Higher Psychological Processes*. Harvard University Press.

Werner, E.E. & Smith, R.S. (2001). *Journeys from Childhood to Midlife: Risk, Resilience, and Recovery*. Cornell University Press.

Wike, T.L. & Fraser, M.W. (2009). School shootings: Making sense of the senseless. *Aggression and Violent Behavior*, 14(3), 162–169.

Wingspread declaration on school connections. (2004). *Journal of School Health*, 74(7), 233–234.

Other sources and further reading

Allen, K.-A., Vella-Brodrick, D. & Waters, L. (2016). Fostering school belonging in secondary schools using a socio-ecological framework. *The Educational and Developmental Psychologist*, 33(1), 97–121.

Allen, K-A. & Boyle, C. (2018). *Pathways to Belonging: Contemporary Research in School Belonging*. Brill Sense.

Baumeister, R.F. & Leary, M.R. (1995). The need to belong: Desire for interpersonal attachments as a fundamental human motivation. *Psychological Bulletin*, 117(3), 497–529.

Catalano, R.F., Haggerty, K.P., Oesterle, S., Fleming, C.B. & Hawkins, J.D. (2004). The importance of bonding to school for healthy development: Findings from the social development research group. *Journal of School Health*, 74(7), 252–261.

Dobia, B., Parada, R., Roffey, S. & Smith, M. (2019). Social and emotional learning: From individual skills to group cohesion. *Educational and Child Psychology*, 36(2), 79–90.

Eisenberger, N.I., Lieberman, M.D. & Williams, K.D. (2003). Does rejection hurt? An fMRI study of social exclusion. *Science, 302*, 290–292.

Lindsay, S. & McPherson, A.C. (2012). Strategies for improving disability awareness and social inclusion of children and young people with cerebral palsy. *Child, Care and Development, 38*(6), 809–816.

McDonald, B., Lester, K. J. & Michelson, D. (2023). 'She didn't know how to go back': School attendance problems in the context of the COVID-19 pandemic—A multiple stakeholder qualitative study with parents and professionals. *British Journal of Educational Psychology, 93*, 386–401.

Roffey, S. (2011). Enhancing connectedness in Australian children and young people. *Asian Journal of School Counselling, 18*(1 & 2), 15–39.

Roffey, S. (2013). Inclusive and exclusive belonging: The impact on individual and community wellbeing. *Educational and Child Psychology, 30*(1), 38–49.

Roffey, S., Boyle, C. & Allen, K-A. (2019). School belonging – Why are our students longing to belong to school? *Educational and Child Psychology, 36*(2), 5–8.

Roffey, S. (2023). ASPIRE to a better future: The impact of the pandemic on young people, and options for schools post-COVID-19. *Education Sciences, 13*, 623.

Rowe, F., Stewart, D. & Patterson, C. (2007). Promoting school connectedness through whole school approaches. *Health Education, 107*(6), 524–542.

Solomon, D., Watson, M., Battistich, V., Schaps, E. & Delucchi, K. (1996). Creating classrooms that students experience as communities. *American Journal of Community Psychology, 24*(6), 719–748.

Thorsborne, M. & Blood, P. (2014). *Implementing Restorative Practices in Schools: A Practical Guide to Transforming School Communities.* Jessica Kingsley.

Weir, K. (2012). The pain of social rejection. *Science Watch, 43*(4), 50. American Psychological Society.

Wilson, D. (2004). The interface of school climate and school connectedness and relationships with aggression and victimization. *Journal of School Health, 74*(7), 293–299.

Resources

The Deliberative Classroom: educateagainsthate.com/resources/the-deliberative-classroom This resource includes videos to stimulate discussions on Islamophobia and the age of criminal responsibility.

neu.org.uk/advice/classroom/behaviour/creating-sense-place-and-belonging-schools

togetherforhumanity.org.au

Twinkl have a list of many cards to start conversations categorised by age twinkl.co.uk/resource/t-l-879-spark-a-conversation-prompt-cards

5 Respect

For individuals, communities and human rights

What do we mean by Respect?

When people are asked to list the qualities of a healthy relationship, Respect frequently comes top of the list. Alongside excellence, it is often referred to in a school's mission statement. But like so many good concepts this principle may stay in the abstract, not always actioned at either the individual or systemic levels, although sometimes there is insistence on Respect for some – especially those in authority.

Universal Respect is treating others as you would wish to be treated – with consideration, kindness and empathy, focusing on individual dignity and our shared humanity. Barack Obama writes about this Golden Rule in his 2006 book, *The Audacity of Hope*:

> *The Golden Rule is not simply a call to sympathy or charity but something more demanding, a call to stand in someone else's shoes and see through their eyes. After all, if (others) are like us, then their struggles are our own. If we fail to help, we diminish ourselves. No-one is exempt from the call to find common ground.*

This principle is explicit in nearly every major religion in the world. Here are a few of them:

- Islam: *No one of you is a believer until you desire for your neighbour that which you desire for yourself.*
- Christianity: *Whatever you wish that others do to you, do so to them.*
- Judaism: *What is hateful to you do not do to your neighbour, that is the basic law, all the rest is commentary.*
- Sikhism: *Do as you desire goodness for yourself as you cannot expect tasty fruits if you sow thorny trees.*
- Hinduism: *This is the essence of morality, do not do to others that which if done to you would cause you pain.*
- Shinto: *The heart of the person before you is a mirror. See there your own form.*

Although Respect is aligned with all the other principles in this book, the two closest are Inclusion and Equity. When power and privilege for some dominate, Respect for others often diminishes. People are treated as disposable, not valuable; as numbers, not salient beings. They cease to matter in their own right, only in terms of what they can deliver or produce.

This chapter explores what Respect looks like and sounds like in practice – for pupils, teachers, schools, families and communities and the difference that it makes when this principle is in place – and when it isn't.

DOI: 10.4324/9781003428244-6

Respect for young people

Respect means valuing the whole person. Every individual is both complex and wonderfully unique. There is a risk that we underestimate young people because we do not tune into their full potential in all the dimensions of their development and learning. These dimensions include cognitive, social, emotional, psychological, language, spiritual, creative, and physical. Teachers who work in target-driven schools may only respect aspects of individuals that tick academic boxes. When someone is tempted to think 'this kid will never learn', they might consider all the things they have already learnt to do. For some just getting to school every day is an achievement.

Respect4us

At "Respect4us", our alternative education provision in Norfolk, we proved over and over again that there is no young person, however traumatised or broken their family background or bad their prior experience of school, who cannot eventually come to believe in themselves, their own value and future. This is achieved through careful observation and listening, reflection with other professionals, endless patience and total respect.

The British deputy prime minister resigned following publication of a report criticising him for bullying civil servants. The independent investigator concluded he had acted in a way that was intimidating and had been "*unreasonably and persistently aggressive*" in meetings. The findings also said his conduct across different government departments "*involved an abuse or misuse of power in a way that undermines or humiliates*". In his resignation letter and subsequent interviews, the minister aired his belief that managers should be free to 'robustly criticise' as a means of driving better performance.

All the evidence indicates the opposite. We do our best work when we are listened to, feel appreciated and valued and are encouraged. We are motivated when our manager, leader or teacher has due regard for our feelings, background, ideas, beliefs, and culture; in short, when our boss shows us respect.

Nowhere is this more the case than in schools. The successful teacher is the one who listens, responds and adapts to the needs of the pupil. The successful school has a culture of respect from top to bottom that is modelled by senior managers – with staff as well as students.

Dominic Boddington MBE is co-author with Liz Easton of **Respect: Stories of troubled children in an alternative educational provision**.

I interviewed students at this provision, and one of the questions asked was the difference between their previous mainstream school and Respect4Us. This included a 15-year-old girl who had many adverse childhood experiences and was now 'looked after' by the local authority. She told me in ways that cannot be described here (!) how she felt she had been treated in her secondary school by many, though not all, teachers who only talked about her unacceptable behaviour. 'Here,' she said, 'they love you'.

Respect for educators

Teaching used to be a profession that was held in high regard. This is still the case in many countries. In Finland, for instance, every teacher has a master's degree and, as the education system is based on trust rather than external controls, teachers have high levels of autonomy. They work within an ethical code based on the principles of dignity, truthfulness, fairness, responsibility and freedom (cited in Tirri & Kuusisto, 2022):

- Dignity means respect for humanity. Teachers are expected to respect every person, regardless of their gender, sexual orientation, appearance, age, religion, social standing, origin, opinions, abilities and achievements.
- Honesty with oneself and with others alongside mutual respect in all communication is a basic aspect of teachers' work. When helping learners navigate life and their environment, they need to be guided by the truth.
- Fairness is important both when encountering individual learners and groups and also in the work community. Fairness involves, in particular, promoting equality and non-discrimination and avoiding favourites.

Finland is acknowledged as having one of the best education systems in the world, with consistently high rankings in the Organisation for Economic Cooperation and Development (OECD) countries and the highest rate of school completion anywhere.

Although many individual teachers are valued members of their communities, Respect for teachers as a body has been undermined in the UK and elsewhere. High-stakes testing has often led to teachers focusing primarily on academic results within a narrow curriculum, as it is this on which they are judged. Respect has also been undermined by a punitive inspection system that can on occasion lead to a decline in mental health for school leaders and an exodus of compassionate teachers. Even though positive interactions may make all the difference to a student's belief in themselves and overall wellbeing, this is rarely acknowledged as a significant part of the role of an educator.

Respect for diverse communities

An inclusive school culture is one where students and their families feel comfortable being themselves and not subject to disrespect and discrimination. Students have an identity based in the communities they come from. In a school this may include several different ethnic, racial or religious groups. When a community is accepted without prejudice or judgment, children are able to be proud of who they are and where they come from and more likely to also feel connected to school. It promotes mutual understanding when the curriculum addresses issues that are relevant to diverse cultures. Students learning about each other broadens their knowledge base and gives them insights into alternative ways of thinking and being. Respect is also encapsulated in asking community members what is important to them and listening carefully to the answers.

There is more on this in Chapter 4 on Inclusion.

Self-respect

Treating others respectfully depends to some extent on self-respect. This is different from self-esteem, which is about how you feel about yourself. As can be seen from toxic leadership, it is possible to have high self-esteem and still put others down. Self-respect is the basis of integrity. It is when you know what your human values are and behave in accordance with these. When this happens, you are less likely to be distressed by unfair criticism or swayed by negative influences. You are confident in who you are, which also means you are able to admit mistakes and ask for help. Self-respect enables you to make decisions based on the values you hold rather than what is expedient or will please others.

Why Respect matters

Congruence with the United Nations Convention on the Rights of the Child

Article 2: Respect for the views of the child: Every child has the right to express their views, feelings and wishes in all matters affecting them, and to have their views considered and taken seriously. This right applies at all times, for example during immigration proceedings, housing decisions or the child's day-to-day home life.

Article 28: Discipline in schools must respect children's dignity and their rights.

Article 29: Goals of education: Education must develop every child's personality, talents and abilities to the full. It must encourage the child's respect for human rights, as well as respect for their parents, their own and other cultures, and the environment.

Respect is treating someone with consideration, care and dignity, alongside due regard for their context. It is honouring their presence, listening to what they have to say, and showing interest. It is treating them as an equal and ensuring that they have what they need to fully participate. This includes acknowledgement of time, work and family issues. Someone who is respected will be more likely to show respect to others. Being singled out for criticism, or being lectured, never makes anyone feel good about either themselves or the person being disrespectful.

Respect fosters collaboration to reach mutually agreed goals. It promotes a culture of trust and high social capital. Disrespectful behaviours build toxic environments which foster a spiral of unhealthy relationships.

Respect in practice in the secondary classroom

Teaching and learning

John Hattie, in his meta-analysis of effective education (2008), talks about having respect for students and their ideas. He says that it is not the extent of teacher subject knowledge that raises attainment but knowing how to introduce new content in a way that integrates this with students' prior knowledge. He concludes that teachers need to talk less and listen more! Listening allows the teacher to learn about the students' prior achievement and understanding. Listening demonstrates respect by showing interest, finding out important information and promoting more effective dialogue. It models reciprocity and respect for the students' perspectives. By listening, teachers model deep communication skills more than just the transmission of knowledge.

Teacher–student relationships

When a young person's efforts to communicate have been met with interest and their initiatives have led to approval, it is easier for them to take risks with their learning. It is more helpful to position someone as 'attention needing' rather than 'attention-seeking'. Establishing and maintaining positive relationships can make a significant difference to student's self-concept, their willingness to listen and their engagement with learning. Here are some ways to do this:

- Welcome students by name if possible.
- Give bite-sized attention. Find out something not to do with school – such as pets, siblings or teams they follow. Circle Solutions sessions facilitate accessing this knowledge in a safe way. Follow up in brief conversations: "*Your team did well on Saturday*", "*Have you heard the new release by...?*"

- Busy teachers don't have much time to listen to pupils, so when opportunities do arise the listening needs to be active. This means acknowledging what is being said, validating associated feelings and asking for clarification when needed (see below).
- Positive relationships are less likely to be fostered with bland praise but with specific feedback, especially when it is aligned with an emerging strength.
- Those who already have a low sense of self find criticism hard to take. It is easier for them if the ratio of positive to negative comments is about 5 to 1. For example, "*I like the way you…*" or "*I have noticed that…*" or "*Well done for…*".
- A student reprimanded for their behaviour may take this as a signal that they themselves are not liked. Adults need to make it clear that it is the behaviour that is unacceptable, not the person. A respectful response says something positive first, such as "*I have seen you be a supportive, good friend, so this behaviour is not the best of you. What's going on?*"
- When settling down to work is an issue, first remind the student what they are expected to do and ask them to tell you the first thing they are going to do. Then walk away rather than stand over them.

The L.A.T.E.R. framework for respectful listening

Based on Michael Tunnecliffe's original LATE framework.

There are increasing numbers of adolescents experiencing serious mental health crises, some coming to believe that life is not worth living. Many teachers will have experienced this in secondary schools. When young people in distress approach adults for help, however, they rarely find this useful. Unless those adults have received some training in active listening, such as counsellors, they often want to problem-solve for that person or try to cheer them up. With the best will in the world, this simply doesn't help. The following might.

L stands for active LISTENING. Close the door, switch off phones and give the student your full attention. Begin with an open question such as "*What's going on?*" or "*You look very down, how are things?*" Show you are listening by nodding, giving brief encouragement to continue ("*mmm*", "*go on*", "*what then*"), or asking for clarification when you don't understand. Otherwise, do not interrupt, except for acknowledging the seriousness for the student.

A is for ACKNOWLEDGEMENT. The situation and the feelings that the student is experiencing are real for them, and this needs to be acknowledged, not dismissed. Simple statements can show that you are taking the student seriously. "*That is hard*", "*No wonder you feel so down*", "*I am so sorry to hear this*".

T stands for TALKING. This is not an opportunity to give advice or say what happened to you. It begins by asking the student what they have thought of doing or have already tried in resolving the situation. They may give just one answer. Ask them to perhaps think of others — there are always alternative options, including doing nothing or 'wait and see'. It is now reasonable to ask "*Have you thought of…?*" and perhaps add to the list of options. You may want to consider going through the pros and cons of each.

E is for ENCOURAGEMENT to take a safe option. The student may have been focused on just one thing that involves self-harm. They now have an understanding that other options are possible. Before they leave the room, ask them if they can commit to doing something that keeps them safe.

R is for REVIEW – it makes sense to arrange a follow-up meeting to check in on how things have been since your conversation. How soon that is may depend on how worried you are about the student's safety and level of depression but should not be more than a few days.

As students are more likely to speak with peers than with adults and young people often don't know how to help, it makes sense for all teenagers to learn this framework so they have a strategy should a friend be in need.

Rudeness and disrespect

Pupils model their behaviour on experiences at home and what they have seen or heard in the media or on the street. Although abusive language is now commonplace, it is still unacceptable for this to be directed at individuals. Some students may resort to abuse towards a teacher when they perceive a threat to their sense of self in some way – perhaps being asked to do a piece of work that they do not believe they have the knowledge or skills for or believe they are being treated unfairly. Teachers have choices when this happens, even though their emotional response may trigger some knee-jerk reactions. Going on the defensive or arguing with a student are never successful strategies and often fuel the situation, making things worse. Saying "*You can't talk to me like that*" is unlikely to be effective either.

Maintaining self-respect means not taking this behaviour personally and staying calm. Easier said than done, but a supportive and emotionally literate school culture that recognises why pupils behave the way they do will help. Modelling courtesy throughout the school is also useful.

If you have built a positive relationship with this pupil, one or more of the following responses may reduce the tension in this situation:

- *This is unacceptable. I treat you with respect, and I expect the same from you.*
- *Take a break and come back and talk to me when you have calmed down.*
- *Did you mean to be rude to me, or are you just upset?* (Sometimes students can be surprised by how their behaviour is interpreted.)
- *That might be OK when you are talking with friends but not with me now.*
- *How else might you say this so I can hear you properly?*

Sometimes rudeness can be the last straw in a difficult day. Rather than react at the time, you might say "*I am finding your behaviour disrespectful and distressing, so I am going to walk away now and talk to you later about this*". This also models good practice.

Respect in practice across the secondary school

Respectful leadership

Despite beliefs that autocratic practices focused on achieving targets are what is needed in schools, there is now a considerable body of research on effective leadership that indicates that it is the soft skills that empower and motivate staff, leading to better learning and well-being outcomes for all.

Scott (2003) ranked the qualities of effective school leaders as:

1 Emotional intelligence: this includes staying calm, keeping things in perspective and maintaining a sense of humour.

2   Social intelligence, including dealing effectively with conflict situations, being able to empathise and work productively with people from a wide range of backgrounds, respecting and honouring diversity. a willingness to listen to different points of view before making decisions and contributing positively to team projects.

3   Intellectual abilities, including identifying priorities and being flexible. Generic and specific skills covered having a clear justified vision for the school and being able to organise and manage time effectively.

Whether they are public or private, formal or informal, it is the everyday conversations that make the difference to levels of trust and respect and critically how people feel in the workplace. Positive organisational psychologists Dutton & Spreitzer (2014) refer to high quality connections as those that

• listen attentively to what people have to say
• are constructively responsive
• make requests rather than demands
• are task-enabling
• show trust by relying on others to meet their commitments
• encourage playfulness.

Although the minutiae of interactions can build either high social capital or a toxic environment, policies embedded in respect make a difference to expectations and outcomes. School leaders are instrumental in this, as illustrated in the Families First case study below. Although this is set in a primary school, it is included here because it is applicable across sectors.

Families First

As a Headteacher, my job is to look after the staff, so that they can look after the children. When staff experience personal challenges such as divorce, sickness, bereavement or other family issues that are clearly affecting their work, we head for the Staff Wellbeing Policy, rather than threatening them with sanctions. We consider how we can hold people through their challenges, keeping the long-term goal of their personal thriving at heart. This includes prioritising time for the staff member and creating safe spaces for them to feel seen and heard without judgment.

Within this space, trust is built for staff to be honest about how they are feeling and any negative impact on their work. We then explore solutions together. These may include additional class support, more PPA time (Preparation, Planning and Assessment), facilitating a reduction of hours or a block of paid leave. Sometimes holding a space for personal reflection is enough. There may be a short-term cost, but over time, individual stories create a staff team who collectively know they are held in unconditional love when life gets tough and consequently go above and beyond for the children once they are back on track. Treating staff with respect and care means that they stay in our school and our profession.

Tina Farr, Headteacher, St. Ebbe's Primary School, Oxford

Transformational leaders able to 'turn schools around' are emotionally literate and put a high value on positive relationships. The sustainability of change depends on the level of trust that permeates a school. Bryk and Sneider (2002) identified this as respect, competence, personal regard for others and integrity. High levels of trust between adults in a school predict higher student academic outcomes.

Respect for teachers

Although pay is one reason for teacher attrition, it is not the only one. Teachers routinely cite stress, overload, working conditions, lack of support from leadership, dealing with challenging pupil behaviour, little autonomy and not feeling valued. It is the accumulation of issues over time, eventually triggered by something specific that prompts a teacher to walk away (DfE, 2018). For education systems to function well educators need to be respected for their knowledge, professionalism and effort. Educators, like students, are multi-dimensional beings and not simply cogs in a machine. For pupils to flourish we must cherish their teachers.

Students who have experienced trauma do not leave their experiences behind when in class. Teachers may find themselves facing the challenges that these young people present on a daily basis. Respect for teachers does not lie in student compliance but in a support system which helps them navigate these challenges. Research indicates how psychologically demanding it is to contain other people's trauma (McCann & Pearlman, 1990), but unlike other professionals such as social workers or psychologists, teachers in the UK do not have regular formal support to manage their emotional response to these situations. Alongside a school environment that offers emotional and physical safety to all members of its community, a supportive, trauma-informed supervision framework is crucial to retaining and motivating classroom teachers and affording them the psychological safety and respect they deserve (McNally, 2022).

Mutual Respect between home and school

Even though the wellbeing and learning of young people is optimally a joint enterprise between home and school, this is rarely played out in practice, especially in secondary schools. Families blame schools when things for their child do not go well, and schools can easily look to parents/carers when teenagers do not comply with learning or behavioural expectations. Mutual respect can be hard to develop and even more challenging to maintain.

It is useful to clearly communicate the school's priorities when a student is first registered. If the wellbeing of the whole person is as important as their learning, setting this out early and often, and explaining why, may help to defer potential conflicts. Also, clarifying when teachers are available for a conversation and when they are not can reduce stress for staff trying to be everything to everyone. This also applies to email and text contact.

Families are not homogenous and may not conform to the traditional nuclear unit. There may be a single parent looking after one or more children, or two parents of the same sex may be co-parenting with a third adult. Other carers may be significant. In Aboriginal communities, for instance, grandparents often raise the children – and in traditional indigenous culture every woman accepts mothering responsibilities with the children in the community.

It is easy to jump to conclusions about families when learning, development, and especially behaviour are not what is expected or wanted in school. Parents, often mothers, can easily be negatively positioned as uncaring. A more respectful starting point is to assume that parents usually want the best for their children and do the best they can with the skills, knowledge, support and resources available to them – this includes emotional resources.

Parents who are demanding and appear aggressive may feel they have to 'fight' for their child. Their experience with authority may so far have left them feeling angry and helpless, and a teacher may be seen as just another authority figure. Acknowledging their parental role as protector and defender makes for a better beginning to a conversation than confrontation. It is then worth saying something positive and caring about the young person, showing that you too have their best interests at heart. Schools are restricted by policies and resources and unlikely to be able to agree with everything parents want, but by respecting their right to ask, listening to their views and explaining what is and is not possible it may be possible to reach agreements. Monitoring outcomes matters, so on-going communication at a level that works for everyone is valuable, perhaps a weekly phone call until the end of term or even better an occasional text saying what has been achieved in either learning or behaviour.

See Chapter 2 on Safety for what to do if a parent comes into school under the influence of drugs or alcohol, or is aggressive or verbally abusive.

Respectful meetings

Meetings are often where the minutiae of respectful interactions are demonstrated – or not. Sometimes those calling the meeting have an agenda where they want to achieve certain outcomes and give lip service to consultation. Respect, however, is encapsulated in active listening; it goes beyond smiling at people to maximising participation so everyone feels they have been heard and their views matter. When this happens, the decisions made are more likely to be enacted. When people leave a meeting feeling side-lined there is little motivation to cooperate. The following outlines good practice.

Invitation

When inviting families for meetings about an individual pupil for whom there is concern, check out when would be a good time for them and invite them as experts on their child. Suggest they bring a friend or other family member – this person is not only there for support at the time but also for talking things over afterwards. Discussing a child's difficulties can be emotional, and people may miss information if they are feeling overwhelmed.

Information

Make the purpose of the meeting clear to everyone and ensure that all participants have the information they need beforehand rather than being given papers as they arrive. Ensure that families can access this information. Not everyone can read or speak the language of the school. Spell out any acronyms and explain what words mean where necessary. There is an educators' vocabulary, and it is easy to make assumptions that people understand what terms like curriculum or pedagogy mean. When I first went to New South Wales, people talked about ISTBs; I had no idea what this meant, and it took a while to summon up the courage to ask and find that it stood for 'Itinerant Support Teacher for Behaviour'. And I then had to look up 'Itinerant' to discover it means travelling from place to place!

The room

Sometimes families need to bring a younger child with them. Having some activities and books available shows you have considered their needs. Setting chairs in a circle means everyone can see and hopefully hear each other and puts everyone on the same level.

Chairing

Suggest that each person introduces themselves, including their role. If staff are called by their first name, that option needs to be given to everyone. The chairperson sets the tone of the meeting, and it helps to begin by saying something positive about the student. Their role is also to make sure that the important issues are discussed, and everyone has the opportunity to contribute. This may mean both listening respectfully but also gently reminding the more dominant voices that others also need to have their say. Keeping the discussion solution-focused rather than dissecting problems is not always easy but is a much better use of people's valuable time. Give time for questions and clarification.

Timings

It helps to be clear about when a meeting will start and when it will end – and stick to these timings. This is being considerate of other commitments people may have. Both families and teachers will be distracted and lose focus if the meeting goes over time.

Interruptions

Ask everyone to switch phones off or to silent. And minimise potential interruptions. These give the impression that other things are more important than the meeting taking place.

Recording

Ask everyone if it is OK to record the main points in writing so everyone can have feedback about what was decided.

At the end

Five minutes before the end of the meeting, the chairperson summarises the main points that have been discussed, especially any agreed actions. Check if anyone wants to add anything, set a review date if appropriate, and then thank everyone for coming.

Rights Respecting Schools

It is valuable for learners to know what their rights are as described in the United Nations Convention on the Rights of the Child (UNCROC), as this also gives them an understanding of their responsibilities in standing up for their own rights and those of others. These are the four guiding principles:

- Non-discrimination (Article 2)
- Best interest of the child (Article 3)
- Right to life survival and development (Article 6)
- Right to be heard (Article 12).

The Rights Respecting Schools Award is a UNICEF initiative. The organisation works with schools to put young people's rights at the centre of policy and practice in the school and create safe and inspiring places to learn, where students are respected, their talents are nurtured, and they are able to thrive. These four standards contribute towards this:

1 *Rights-respecting values underpin leadership and management*
   The best interests of the child are a top priority in all actions. Leaders are committed to placing the values and principles of UNCROC at the heart of all policies and practice.
2 *The whole school community learns about UNCROC*
   The Convention is made known to students and adults. Young people and adults use this shared understanding to work for global justice and sustainable living.

3   *The school has a rights-respecting ethos*
    Young people and adults collaborate to develop and maintain a rights-respecting school community, based on UNCROC, in all areas and in all aspects of school life.
4   *Children and young people are empowered to become active citizens and learners*
    Every child has the right to say what they think in all matters affecting them and to have their views taken seriously. Young people develop the confidence, through their experience of an inclusive rights-respecting school community, to play an active role in their own learning and to speak and act for the rights of all to be respected locally and globally.

A Rights Respecting School

At Balerno High School we recently achieved our Gold Rights Respecting Schools Award (RRSA). Participating in the award has had a hugely positive impact on our school. We have seen a big increase in the number of pupils wanting to get involved in projects and groups across the school to work on issues that matter to them. From the point of view of our RRSA staff leads, the biggest change has been the transition from having pockets of pupil voice across the school to now seeing pupils leading change and driving forward improvement in the school. Our pupil RRSA team have also shared what they think the biggest impact of the Rights Respecting Schools Award has been. One of our RRSA members said, *"It has boosted my confidence and made me more aware of the rights I am entitled to."* Another said, *"It has made the school more welcoming. Being a member of the RRSA has given me the chance to work with pupils in different year groups."* Our school's Pupil Parliament RRSA representative said, *"RRSA has created a more inclusive environment in the school where pupils can get involved with projects and activities. Becoming a Gold Rights Respecting School has allowed more pupils to feel they have a say in decisions about things that are happening in the school."* Finally, when asked how they would describe their experiences of the Rights Respecting Schools Award in one word, members from our RRSA team said *"fun"*, *"inclusive"*, *"life changing"* and *"amazing!"*

Written by Balerno High School's Rights Respecting Schools Award Team

---

The impact of Rights Respecting Schools appears to be far-reaching (UNICEF, 2016). An evaluation of over 500 schools in England, Wales, Scotland and Northern Ireland indicated that between 93% and 98% of Headteachers considered that being a Rights Respecting School enhanced pupil respect for themselves and others, improved relationships and behaviour, saw young people more engaged with learning, and led to more positive attitudes towards diversity. 76% reported a decrease in bullying and exclusions.

Respect for diverse communities

It is easy to jump to conclusions about other people based on limited information and stereotypes. How people dress and speak, their marital status, home circumstances, religion and profession can quickly lead to assumptions about expectations, motivations, intentions, values and possibilities. Communication and actions can then be based on misinformation, which can create unnecessary difficulties rather than opening up options for resolving issues. One parent was told by a teacher that she thought her son had problems in school because she was a single mother! The only way to avoid this sort of disrespect is to resist making judgments, but instead to ask questions to ascertain useful information.

Respect for diverse cultures is demonstrated in what is seen and heard around a school. When some of the staff in a school also come from the communities the school serves, this also gives positive messages about the value of that community.

Signs and communications need to be in community languages, and interpreters available when needed.

Respect and culture

As the new wellbeing person at a high school, I left my office door ajar to signal I was open to conversation. Very soon two girls invited themselves in and sat down next to my desk. They had just arrived from a remote community in Central Australia. *"Hello,"* I said. *"Where you from?"* they asked. I named the suburb in which I lived and explained, *"it's over in that direction, on a special hill,"* thinking that would help to give them a better sense of location. *"But where you from?"* was the response.

Then it dawned on me. Where you are from in Warlpiri culture does not refer to an address. It is about where a person belongs, the land where they and their kin have ancestral ties. The girls were seeking to understand who I was according to their cultural lore, which determines how relationships and communications should proceed.

Cultural psychologist Richard Shweder once observed that when people from different cultures meet 'there is no neutral place to stand'. Deeply embedded cultural assumptions shape our bearing, our relationships and our institutions. For someone identified with the dominant worldview of the coloniser those girls might be judged confused, or perhaps insolent.

Unfortunately, many young First Nations students in Australian schools experience this kind of treatment. In a system that does not recognise what they have to offer they are not afforded the kind of respect that is demanded of them. Before demanding respect, let's first understand what being respectful means. Respect starts with listening. Listening deeply and respectfully changes hearts and grows mutual understanding.

Dr Brenda Dobia, co-author of Respect for Culture – Social and Emotional Learning with Aboriginal and Torres Strait Islander Youth. **In Martin, Frydenberg & Collie (Eds.) Social and Emotional Learning in Australia and the Asia-Pacific**.

Behaviour

The language of disorders and a respectful alternative

There used to be schools in the UK for 'maladjusted children'. Those students were not 'maladjusted' – they were adjusting to the circumstances and experiences that had shaped them. The label of 'maladjusted' placed the problem squarely within the pupil and indicated that they were the ones who had to change. This is also true of many psychiatric 'disorders'. The *Diagnostic and Statistical Manual of Mental Disorders* (5th ed.) lists at least 157, some of which are simply descriptions of behaviours for which there is little biological / chemical basis. There is considerable controversy about this deficit psychiatric approach, although it is often taken as a 'given' in popular media.

The British Psychological Society has developed an alternative framework for exploring a student's difficulties. Instead of looking at what is 'wrong' with someone, it asks the question "What has happened?" to them and what impact has this had. This is called the Power, Threat, Meaning Framework and can be accessed from the link in the References.

Sometimes it is hard, if not impossible, to know what has been happening in a young person's life. Schools often don't have the time or resources to find out a student's history or circumstances. It makes sense, however, to begin with the premise that a young person who is acting up has a reason for this. Pupils need to know what is and is not acceptable in school and not be a danger to themselves or others, but otherwise it makes sense to treat every young person with care and respect. There are many biographies where individuals who have made a success of their lives despite challenging circumstances and defiant behaviour in school attribute this to the support of a teacher who treated them with kindness. Teachers make more difference than they know.

Respect in social and emotional learning (SEL)

Respect in Circle Solutions is summarised by 'we listen to each other'. This means that when it is one person's turn to speak, often signalled by holding the 'talking stick' (which can be an unplugged microphone or similar), others do not interrupt or speak amongst themselves. If that happens, the facilitator stops everything and waits until the talking stops. They may use a 'proximal praise' strategy by thanking the person nearest the talkers for waiting quietly. Respect is also activated by the 'no put downs' guideline. Participants may say 'personal positives' to each other, but statements that demean someone are not acceptable. This extends to derogatory non-verbal expressions – such as raising your eyebrows at what someone has said.

Activities in SEL

The following activity enables students to understand the concept of respect more fully.

Strengths in Circles cards

The Strengths in Circles cards have seven statements on Respect for students to discuss in small groups. The ones most suitable for secondary students are:

* We are all unique.
* We value differences.
* We give and receive feedback respectfully.
* We listen to each other.

Students are in random groups of three or four: for each phrase they are asked to discuss:

– What does this mean?
– How would we see / hear this in action?
– Do we want this in our school? Why?
– Is there anything we could we do to have more of this?

It is not necessary for all these questions to be given at the same time. When they take place over successive Circle sessions this gives pupils opportunities to identify and think about what is happening in their school and how it makes them feel.

Trust

Trust is an aspect of Respect and similar activities can help young people understand what it means in practice. For example:

If Trust came into this classroom today, what would we notice? What would we see and hear? What would people be feeling? What might someone feel when Trust isn't there?
  In pairs, talk about and then finish these sentences:

– *"Trust is when ..."*
– *"Being able to trust someone means ..."*
– *"We can be trustworthy by ..."*

Hypotheticals

Small groups talk about these situations and decide what would be a respectful thing to do and why.

1   A family board a bus. There are two children aged about five and eight and a mother who is carrying a baby. The two children run to sit on the only seat available.
2   A homeless person is in a doorway, covered by a blanket. Two teenagers come past and take a pack of sandwiches that someone has left for the homeless person.
3   A new member of staff walks with a limp. Some pupils follow him up the corridor, mimicking his walk and laughing.

Respect checklist

	This is in place – we know it is effective because …	Working on it – our actions to date are …	Just started – our next step will be …
All staff have discussed and defined Respect and self-Respect.			
Respect is modelled in all interactions.			
Courtesy is modelled and encouraged.			
Staff are skilled in active listening.			
There is a 'no put down' policy across the school.			
Meetings are respectful.			
People trust each other.			
The school is 'Rights Respecting'.			
Behaviour is seen as communication.			
Pupils have been learning about Respect in SEL			

Respect in the future

Every day we hear of behaviour that demeans others, often from people who are in positions of authority and who are employed to take care of the welfare of others. Those being abused or denigrated are invariably vulnerable in some way – asylum seekers, mentally ill, children, ethnic minorities, the elderly and women, especially when alone.

Although it is a minority who behave this way, there is continuing reluctance in calling them out. Respect is also due to those who are prepared to put themselves on the line as opponents of this behaviour.

If we are to build a society where Respect for others is part of the fabric of daily life, then every student should experience Respect at school and learn what it means from the day they enter until the day they leave. A one-off lesson in respectful relationships is better than nothing but is nowhere near enough. Respect needs to be threaded through the learning environment for everyone.

References, further reading and resources

Boddington, D. & Easton, L. (2021). *Respect: Stories of Troubled Children in an Alternative Educational Provision*. Published by the authors.

British Psychological Society: *Power, Threat, Meaning Framework* bps.org.uk/member-networks/division-clinical-psychology/power-threat-meaning-framework

Bryk, A. & Sneider, B. (2002). *Trust in Schools*. Russell Sage.

Department for Education (2018). *Factors Affecting Teacher Retention. Qualitative investigation. Research report*. Cooper Gibson Research.

Dutton, J.E. & Spreitzer, G.M. (Eds.). (2014). *How to be a Positive Leader: Small Actions, Big Impact*. Berrett-Koehler.

Hattie, J. (2008). *Visible Learning: A Meta-Analysis of Over 800 Meta-Analyses Relating to Achievement*. Routledge.

McCann, I.L. & Pearlman, L.A. (1990). Vicarious traumatization: A framework for understanding the psychological effects of working with victims. *Journal of Traumatic Stress, 3*, 131–149.

McNally, S. (2022). *Using Hermeneutic Phenomenology and Visual Representation to Explore Trauma in the Primary Classroom: The Case for Classroom Teachers to Access Supervision*. Unpublished thesis.

Obama, B. (2006). *The Audacity of Hope*. Crown/Three Rivers Press.

Scott, G. (2003). *Learning Principals - Leadership Capability & Learning*. University of Technology, Sydney. Commissioned Research for NSW DET., March, 2003.

Tirri, K. & Kuusisto, E. (2022). *Teachers' Professional Ethics: Theoretical Frameworks and Empirical Research from Finland*. Brill.

UNICEF. (2016). *Research on rights respecting schools*. unicef.org.uk/rights-respecting-schools/the-rrsa/impact-of-rrsa/evidence_2016

Other sources and further reading

Children's Society. childrenssociety.org.uk/what-we-do/our-work/supporting-young-carers/facts-about-young-carers

Cole, T. (2010). Ease practitioner stress to improve services for children and young people with SEBD. *Emotional and Behavioural Difficulties, 15*(1), 1–4.

Gerhardt, S. (2015). *Why Love Matters: How Affection Shapes a Baby's Brain*. 2nd ed. Routledge.

Johnson, L. & Boyle, M. (2020). *A Straight Talking Introduction to the Power Threat Meaning Framework: An Alternative to Psychiatric Diagnosis*. PCCS Books.

Rae, T. (2012). Developing emotional literacy approaches for staff and students. Developing an approach in an SEBD school. In J. Visser, H. Daniels, T. Cole, & C. Forlin (Eds.), *Transforming Troubled Lives: Strategies and Interventions for Children with Social, Emotional, and Behavioural Difficulties. International Perspectives*. Emerald.

Roffey, S. (2002). *Schools Behaviour and Families: Frameworks for Working Together*. Routledge.

Roffey. S. (2005). *Respect in Practice – The challenge of emotional literacy in education. Conference paper ROF05356*. Australian Educational Research.

Roffey, S. (2007). Transformation and emotional literacy: The role of school leaders in developing a caring community. *Leading and Managing*, *13*(1), 16–30.

Roffey, S. (2012). Pupil wellbeing: Teacher wellbeing: Two sides of the same coin? *Educational and Child Psychology*, *29*(4), 8–17.

Roffey, S. & Parry, J. (2013). *Special Needs in the Early Years: Promoting Collaboration, Communication and Co-Ordination*. 3rd ed. Routledge.

Resources

Equality and Human Rights Commission: This report shows how schools have implemented Human Rights Education across England, Scotland and Wales: equalityhumanrights.com/en/publication-download/exploring-human-rights-education-great-britain

UNICEF: The Rights Respecting School Award: unicef.org.uk/rights-respecting-schools/the-rrsa/

TEDx Talk by Sue Roffey: *School as Family*: youtube.com/watch?v=XaHOQ9DmffE

6 Equity

Fairness and flexibility

What do we mean by Equity?

Equality has benefits for both individuals and society. The least gap between the privileged and the poor in any country promotes higher levels of wellbeing. But for all students to do well in education, we must think differently from the 'one size fits all' approach, as this clearly does not work for everyone. For young people to have equal opportunities to flourish and learn, we need both education policy and schools to be adaptable, flexible and fair. This is the basis of Equity.

There are several ways in which students may be disadvantaged – many of these interact with each other. Most of the time the focus is on poverty, race or geography, but the list here shows that there is no such thing as the typical or 'normal' student and that the factors that influence pupil attainment are many and varied.

Socio-economic factors

The impact of poverty was writ large in the pandemic, when pupils were expected to learn at home. Not all had the technology they needed, and living in cramped accommodation meant they did not have the space to study. Poverty also negatively affects nutrition, warmth, sleep, security, mental health and relationships. When young people have such challenges at home, school can become a lifeline with the provision of basic needs, access to the internet, after-school activities, and people who show they care.

Social factors

Inequity is associated with discrimination, where there are prejudiced expectations of certain groups related to race, class, language, religion, gender or disability. This is particularly the case for indigenous and migrant communities everywhere. Some subjects still have a gender bias, and in many countries girls are denied equal access to education, an issue that was exacerbated during the pandemic.

Family factors

Some individuals may live in dysfunctional or abusive households, where they get little educational support or encouragement. Parents may not value education themselves, and even if they do want their children to do well they do not have the knowledge or resources to support them. In other more economically advantaged homes, some families are so focused on being successful that they do not foster the relational environment that enables young people to thrive.

DOI: 10.4324/9781003428244-7

Being in care

In 2001, 44 children in every ten thousand in the UK were 'looked after' by local authorities. By 2022 that figure had nearly doubled to over 70. The total for 2023 is up 2% on the previous year with almost 84,000 individuals in care with over half young people aged over 10 (Gov UK 2023). Those who are 'looked after' have a range of poor outcomes, including lower educational attainments, poorer physical and mental health, and involvement with juvenile justice. As adults they are more likely to face stark health and socio-economic inequalities in the years and decades after (Sacker et al., 2021).

Being a young carer

As many as 1 in 5 children are carers for someone in their family who is sick, disabled or has mental health or addiction problems. It is estimated that there are over 820,000 carers between the ages of 11 and 16 in England alone (Children's Society, 2023). These young people are likely to miss up to 25% of their schooling. Two thirds of young carers do not inform schools of their situation.

Loss

Although rarely acknowledged in schools as an impediment to wellbeing and learning, many young people struggle, at least temporarily, with the absence of significant people in their lives. Bereavement is usually a more straightforward loss than family breakdown, but for both the impact will depend on how close someone was to the person they have lost. Nearly half of all young people in Western countries are living with one parent by the time they are 16. Even though family breakdown is a common occurrence it still has a profound impact on individuals. Depending on age, prior levels of conflict, and how the breakdown has been mediated, responses can range from relief, confusion, rejection and anger to sadness and fear for the future. It is not unusual for young people to express strong emotions at school rather than at home, and unless adults find out what is happening, behavioural problems can escalate. This can also happen with reconstituted families when teenagers have to adapt to new people being around, sometimes with little or no negotiation or involvement in that decision.

Disability

Although some children have disabilities that require formal assessment and specified intervention, such as in an Education, Health and Care Plan (UK), many more need adaptations and/or support to fully access the curriculum. This includes hearing loss, poor eyesight, problems with the printed word, sequencing, organisational skills and more.

Cultural and language factors

School systems, values and expectations may be different from the home culture, and this can lead to misunderstandings and a lack of collaboration that disadvantages pupils. Students who are newly arrived may have skills and abilities that are not immediately evident because they are coping with major changes in their lives, learning a new language, trying to fit in and learn 'how things happen' in their new environment. It is best to reserve judgment while this process is under way. Although individuals invariably learn a second language at school over time, they may need visual and contextual support whilst working towards fluency.

Geographic factors

In some areas funding cuts to local authorities have meant that schools themselves are disadvantaged, with poor infrastructure, inadequate resources and sometimes lack of staff. In some of the poorest areas, schools have had to rely on charities to give pupils breakfast before they come to class and have secured warm clothing for them in winter.

Trauma

Students who have experienced either incidental or chronic trauma may not be able to focus and learn. Amongst other things they may be hypervigilant, sleep-deprived, emotionally volatile and experiencing flashbacks. This takes individuals to a level of distress that is hard both for them and for those trying to teach them. Trauma-informed positive education in these circumstances can support both pupils and educators (Brunzell & Norrish, 2021).

Structural barriers to Equity

There are three overarching issues that impact on equity throughout education. The first is the system in which young people are educated, the second is the curriculum that is on offer and how meaningful this is to students, and the third is learning in a competitive environment where in order to have winners in education some have to be losers. This applies to both students and schools and is particularly relevant in a 'teach to the test' approach, where the definitions of 'success' and school 'excellence' are based primarily and sometimes almost exclusively on final exam results. This cannot provide an education in which the best of each young person is developed and acknowledged.

Alternative education systems

It is not possible to have a chapter on equity in education without referring to the discrimination posed by different systems. Most of the information in this book refers to state education – i.e. not paid for by parents but by local authorities or the government. Of the 8.8 million children and young people in the UK the vast majority go to a state school. The average cost of a private education at the time of writing is nearly £15,000 a year, which means that only those who have a secure high income, inherited wealth, generous relatives, or sacrifice many things themselves can afford this for their children. Parents often do this because they believe it will give their children an advantage in a competitive world. It has, however, become evident in certain echelons of society, not just in the UK, that it is not only the smaller classes, the broader curriculum and the extra tuition to gain a place in a 'good university' that they hope for, but also associating with others who will provide them with 'contacts' later in life. The 'old boys' network' is alive and well, especially in the more elite independent schools, and has significant influence on the availability of opportunities. This maintains and perpetrates inequality and a class system based on wealth and privilege. It is therefore essential that state education has the resources to enable every young person to thrive and fulfil their own potential.

The curriculum

In Chapter 3 on Positivity, we cited evidence for increasing disengagement in high schools, especially in mid-adolescence. A significant proportion of teenagers claim they are often bored. Much of this is due to the continued narrowing of the curriculum in the state system. The national curriculum is also disadvantaging school-leavers, as it is offering neither regional flexibility nor the skills employers say they need – such as team-work, good communication, innovative thinking and practical life-skills. In independent schools, where it is not mandatory to follow the prescribed curriculum, there are many more opportunities for students to engage in learning by developing their strengths and interests, including arts, dance, drama, music, languages, social action and sports. There are, however, examples of courageous school leaders and teachers in state schools who build what Debra Kidd describes as a 'curriculum of hope' (2020) by actions such as integrating subjects, engaging in and with local communities, using current events as a basis for subject exploration, making links with social and emotional understanding and encouraging learning outside the classroom.

Competition

When test results are the benchmark on which schools are judged, there is less room for flexibility or for collaboration. Although some assert that competition is motivating, this is only true for those who have the possibility of achieving. Competition can create fear of failure – never being 'good enough' – a phenomenon that has been exacerbated by social media. I once counselled a boy in a high school where they graded pupils according to their yearly test results. He was distressed and depressed because last year he had come second in his class and this year was fourth. He said he was letting his parents down. The only criterion of worth in the mind of this young and able student was how he measured up against others.

Equity is probably the most challenging of the positive education principles to implement but is also the most important for a future thriving society. Although Equity is largely dependent on the socio-cultural-political macro level in an ecological model (Bronfenbrenner, 1979), it is worth remembering that all levels interact with each other bi-directionally, and that systems change over time. Here we explore what we can do at every level to give each young person the best chance to learn and flourish, despite the circumstances into which they were born or what has happened to them since.

Why does Equity matter?

Congruence with the United Nations Convention on the Rights of the Child

Article 29 (goals of education): Education must develop every child's personality, talents and abilities to the full.
Article 23 (children with a disability): A child with a disability has the right to live a full and decent life with dignity and, as far as possible, independence and to play an active part in the community.
Article 39 (recovery from trauma and re-integration): Children who have experienced neglect, abuse, exploitation or torture or are victims of war must receive special support to help them recover their health, dignity, self-respect and social life.

We all start life in differing circumstances – some are born into privilege or as citizens of a nation that looks after people who have fallen on hard times, while others find themselves in families and communities who have very little resources. Some are born surrounded by love, care and support; others less so.

While there has been reduction in global inequality over the last few decades, within-country inequalities have increased, especially in advanced economies. This leads to unwanted consequences, not only for the disadvantaged but also for society as a whole.

Reversing cycles of disadvantage

An overwhelming reason for Equity in positive education is intervening in cycles of disadvantage (Quinlan & Roffey, 2021). Deprivation, with all the disadvantages and hardships this brings for individuals, families, communities and society, is not an inevitable fact of life. The following are just three examples of interventions in the UK that historically reversed cycles of disadvantage.

The welfare state

After the Second World War in Britain, there was a determined effort to create a country fit for all to live in. The welfare state was established and millions of people, especially the post-war generation, benefitted from a new National Health Service, free higher education, and a social security system to help those in need. The impact was significant. Children from previously impoverished households had opportunities beyond their parents' dreams. Upward social mobility enabled more individuals to hold down good jobs, many being the first in their family to go to university and attain a profession, such as teachers, lawyers and doctors. The post-war generation often earned enough to buy their own homes, were free from fear of poverty, and had hope of a brighter future.

The benefits to the nation were immense – but the system was fragile in the face of capitalism and the growing influence of market forces, increasing individualism, and an erroneous 'belief in a just world' (Lerner, 1980). This is the basis of 'the American dream', which says that everyone can 'make it' by their own efforts if they work hard enough. If you are not successful it is deemed to be your fault. This ignores the contexts into which people are born or the life events that might befall them, and risks creating a society lacking in empathy and humanity. When the accumulation of wealth and status is valued more highly than almost anything else, unethical if not criminal behaviour becomes inevitable.

Sure Start

In 1998, with a growing awareness of the vital importance of the early years for life trajectories, the Sure Start programme was initiated across the UK. Child-care centres were established to support young families from pregnancy to when children were four, especially in areas of disadvantage. These provided integrated multi-agency services, including child care and early education programmes, health services, play facilities, parenting classes and specialised family support services. A government evaluation (Gaheer & Paul, 2016) found that overall these provided value for money, although it was not possible to evaluate the longer-term and accumulative impact. There were clear indications, however, of Sure Start intervening in the cycle of disadvantage. The biggest impacts on child health are seen in adolescence. According to research by the Institute of Fiscal Studies (Cattan et al., 2021), around 13,000 admissions of older children to hospital each year were likely prevented by the work of Sure Start children's centres. The evaluation goes on to estimate the positive impact on school attendance and achievement, reduction in crime and anti-social behaviour, reducing smoking and improvements in mental health.

The number of Sure Start centres peaked at around 3,620 in 2010 but with the policy of austerity, funding has been reduced by 60%, with many closed down or offering reduced services. There is now a resurgence of cross-party interest in establishing family centres with similar functions, but currently most initiatives are funded by charities rather than government.

Subsidised higher education

Although there may be some financial support for further education courses, such as technical and applied qualifications for 16- to 19-year-olds, it now costs a great deal to go to a university in the UK to get a degree. This was not the case between 1962 and 1998 when fees were covered, alongside means-tested contributions towards maintenance. This enabled many to study for professions that would previously have been inaccessible to them. Now young people without financial resources go into years of debt to gain higher qualifications. Free or heavily subsidised higher education is, however, available to citizens across the world, including in 11 European countries, including all of the Nordic nations.

Community safety

The term 'structural violence' has been used to define unequal distribution of power and resources said to be built into the structure of a society (Galtung, 1969, 1990). It is more deadly than physical violence perpetrated by individuals, as it stealthily but consistently prevents groups of citizens from having their basic needs met. This leads to economic deprivation, injustice, poor mental and physical health, and often earlier mortality. The resulting resentment and need to find someone to blame can lead to community unrest, conflict and actual violence. It is unsurprising that those in power will point to sections of the community as a justified target, such as refugees, those on benefits, the homeless or ethnic communities. Actual violence is sometimes referred to as the tip of the iceberg in full view and often in the media spotlight, whereas the rest of the iceberg – out of sight – is the structural and cultural violence that enables it. Nelson Mandela is one of many who recognised that while poverty, injustice, and gross inequality persist in society, no-one can 'truly rest'. It follows that policies and practices that promote Equity can boost social cohesion and reduce conflict.

Democracy

We have an education system in many countries that does not adequately prepare young people to be active and engaged citizens in the 21st century. Politicians may rely on voter ignorance or apathy and belief in what they read on social media in order to be elected on platforms that are not always in people's best interests. Lower taxes, for instance, are most advantageous to those who have enough income to benefit, but politicians often refer to what 'the people' want as a unitary concept. Equity as a principle therefore includes citizenship, critical thinking and social justice. Future citizens need to know how their country is run, who makes decisions, what vested interests are, why voting matters and how to differentiate between fact, fiction and opinion.

Collaboration

Competition in education has a wide range of negative consequences. When students are measured against each other there are always going to be winners and losers. This may be fine for those who do well academically, but constant failure is not motivating, and students lose enthusiasm for learning. When education is about enabling each student to become the best of themselves, failure is not on the agenda.

When schools themselves are measured against each other they are less likely to collaborate. Although there is an increasing expectation on schools to support one another to facilitate educational improvement and Equity, the *"English educational system remains a deeply marketised arena in which schools must compete over pupils, funding and resources in order to survive"* (Armstrong et al., 2021).

Collaboration between schools is facilitated by leaders who coordinate together, share responsibility and build capacity. Trust and clear communication foster the relationships that enable people to work together. A pre-existing culture of collaboration is also helpful. Partnerships that flourish have a strong focus on teaching and learning, shared values, dispersed leadership responsibility and a commitment to professional development.

Economic benefits

The Times Education Commission Report: Bringing Out the Best (Sylvester & Seldon, 2022) notes "*the missing geniuses of this generation whose potential is being wasted by a flawed and unfair education system*" and points out that billions may be lost to the economy as a result. Although it is not straightforward to measure, as there are many interacting variables, there are indications that intervention to promote equity in education also saves considerable costs much further down the line in improved health and wellbeing, better employment prospects, stronger and more supportive relationships, and contributions to society.

What is Equity in education?

Equity in education goes beyond supporting students who need it most. It is empowering teachers and school leaders to support a fairer, safer and more democratic society both through and within education.

> *Ultimately it is about supporting informed and well-educated citizens, who are the foundation for stronger economies and more resilient societies of the future.*
>
> (OECD)

Equity refers to the principle of fairness. "*Inequities occur when biased or unfair policies, programmes, practices, or situations contribute to a lack of equality in educational performance, results, and outcomes*" (The Glossary of Education Reform, 2016). Providing Equity in education requires honesty about inequality and its impact on individuals and society in the future. It entails a commitment to those with unique needs and those disadvantaged by systemic inequalities. What we have seen in recent years, and especially since the pandemic, is increasing inequality, and a growing gap in opportunities, attainments and life chances. Although this is happening globally there are pockets of good practice everywhere.

What is happening internationally

Creating equitable provision for diverse student populations is a key feature of education policy in OECD countries. Some countries appear to be doing much better than others. Here are just two of many examples.

Finland

Since the 1980s, Finnish educators have focused on making education an instrument to balance out social inequality. Schools are not in competition with each other for who is 'best' or 'top,' as collaboration is the norm. The aim is to support each other to do well. Pupil progress is tracked individually, with no standardized testing. There are no government inspections that grade schools against specific criteria. Although private education is not banned it is illegal to provide basic education for profit. Finland has consistently better educational outcomes than most across the world.

Estonia

Classes are mixed-ability and pupils are not routinely separated into sets. Exclusions are virtually unheard of, and most young people stay in education until they are 19. Schools are the best at promoting fairness, and Estonian pupils are amongst the happiest in the world. The government trusts teachers and both educators and schools have a high degree of autonomy. There is an emphasis on problem-solving, critical thinking, values, entrepreneurship and digital competence – skills employers want. According to the OECD Programme for International Student Assessment, Estonia has the best education system in Europe.

Equity in practice in the secondary classroom

Equity is when each individual has what they need and the same opportunities for success as others. This means both taking barriers away or putting things in place. In the classroom some students might be given extra time, different supports, or specific resources to maximise their learning outcomes.

Although Equity is largely the responsibility of schools, school systems and educational policies, there are things subject teachers can do to promote flexibility and fairness.

Oracy

It is our ability to communicate that enables us to build positive relationships, collaborate for common purpose, deliberate and share our ideas as citizens. It is through speaking and listening that we develop our views, apply knowledge and extend our capacity to think critically.

(Millard & Menzies, n.d.)

As 75% of UK children who experience poverty come to school with limited language skills, and over half of employers say weak communication skills in school-leavers is one of their greatest challenges, it is imperative that schools, especially in the state sector, focus on developing stronger, more flexible and more fluent verbal communication. Talking is a fundamental skill, but often takes second place to literacy in schools. It has outcomes beyond the classroom that can benefit students far into their future, including positive relationships and work opportunities. A focus on oracy helps students discuss topics with others, explore their understanding, develop confidence in their ideas and present their findings. Even when young people are doing well academically they may lack confidence in sharing their ideas, so a focus on oracy benefits everyone.

The Education Endowment Foundation in conjunction with Sheffield University published research (2017) on 'dialogic teaching' that aimed to improve the quality of classroom talk as a means of increasing pupil engagement, learning and attainment, particularly for those from disadvantaged backgrounds. Although the research was conducted with Year 5 pupils, not high school students, there were significant improvements in attainments in English, science and maths for all students, with pupils entitled to free school meals making additional progress.

Teaching and learning talking

Oracy is not a specific lesson but is threaded through everyday interactions. It is as much about modelling and structured opportunities as direct input. Both the depth and breadth of vocabulary matter. Students need to know what words mean and the contexts in which to use them, and to have access to alternatives that allow them to be more specific in their descriptions and communicate subtlety. Language in the classroom needs to become increasingly sophisticated with new words explained and then used frequently until they become embedded in pupil vocabulary. Oracy is aligned with cooperative learning in that students need to talk to each other to develop and communicate their ideas. When teachers ask for contributions from a whole class it is usually the already confident and able individuals who are most likely to answer. This does not offer opportunities to raise the ability or confidence of others. It is better to have students work in pairs and small groups and then discuss and report on their findings. It is not only verbal content that matters but also how to communicate well in different contexts. Oracy can be promoted in secondary schools by

- Respecting students' ideas
- Giving positive feedback for extending communication skills and taking risks with new vocabulary: this means accepting that mistakes will happen and are positioned as steps to learning
- Clarifying the meanings of words that may not already be in a student's lexicon
- Generating more words to discuss a topic – perhaps using a thesaurus
- Repeating new words and using them in different contexts
- Using drama to good effect – such as different voices in reading aloud
- Posing structured questions for discussion – on issues that have meaning for young people
- Teaching students the basics of good discussion, such as active listening and inviting contributions
- Encouraging debates that deepen knowledge and understanding and promote critical thinking.

Oracy is a powerful tool for learning; by teaching students to become more effective speakers and listeners we empower them to better understand themselves, each other and the world around them. It is also a route to social mobility, empowering all students, not just some, to find their voice to succeed in school and life.

(Voice21)

Demonstrating knowledge

Traditionally students were asked to write individual essays to demonstrate knowledge, but that is very limiting with today's breadth of possibilities. Alternatives may be individual, paired and cooperative group efforts which could include podcasts, videos, power point presentations, info-graphs, drawings, mind-maps, posters or presentations incorporating drama. Technology has developed in multiple ways that allow students to express their ideas without resorting to putting 'pen to paper'. But facilities and technical expertise need to be available to students. This means ensuring that everyone has access to laptops and reliable Wi-Fi both in school and at home, alongside teachers who have the necessary skills and knowledge to support students.

Critical thinking

Students from families who have resources with parents who have probably been to university themselves have more opportunities to learn at home. If school is the main venue through which low socioeconomic status students might be exposed to advanced vocabulary, deep knowledge and demands for higher-level and critical thinking, it is vital for equity that those opportunities be enhanced (OECD, 2019).

The core of critical thinking is reflecting on and questioning what you have been told and the application of this knowledge. It fosters meta-cognition, which can be defined as thinking about your own thinking, including having an awareness of the influences on perceptions and understanding. It is about knowing the difference between fact and opinion and valuing evidence-based information. This is particularly relevant in today's world where social media perpetrates conspiracy theories that undermine both democracy and universal wellbeing. When lies are told with impunity it is hard for people to navigate their worlds effectively.

Critical thinking is a pedagogical approach that can be adopted across the curriculum. It involves analysis, synthesis and evaluation which can mean different things in different disciplines. It has two basic strands: (1) using reason and logic to analyse and evaluate evidence and the positions that others take, and (2) being able to use information to address a wide range of issues.

It can be fostered by reflective journaling, open-ended questions and discussion topics. Closed questions assume that there is only one correct answer which might be true for some subjects but not so much for others. These are a few options for discussion:

- How might we see this issue from different perspectives?
- Is this statement based on fact or opinion – how can we tell?
- In what ways is this learning important?
- In what ways might this learning be applied in different contexts?
- How does the choice of language in this report make us think about it in a certain way?
- What is the difference between correlation (when two things appear connected) and causation (when one thing changes the outcome of another) and why does this matter when we consider evidence?
- If many people believe something, does this make it true? What past beliefs about the world have changed with the advent of science and greater knowledge?
- What other information might we need to understand something? What is missing?

Cooperative learning

This is based on a set of principles and techniques that enable students to effectively collaborate with each other. These include the following:

- Random groupings, so that students collaborate with a wide range of peers – this enriches learning, facilitates new perspectives, and seeks strengths in others
- Teaching basic collaborative skills, such as asking for help, offering suggestions, giving feedback, responding positively to others' ideas and efforts, managing different viewpoints without conflict, following up on suggestions and showing pride in achievements
- Reliance on group members first before asking the teacher
- Equal opportunities to participate – each person has a role and no-one is excluded
- All students are expected to contribute and are accountable to the rest of the group for what they offer to the joint project: no-one can opt out
- Interdependence means that what benefits one person will benefit the group and what is damaging to one pupil affects the group
- Cooperation is seen as a value that improves the lives of individuals, groups, whole communities and society.

Collaborative activities could include research, project development, and presentation to the class.

When students use collaborative skills, their groups are likely to function better (Soller, 2001), leading to more learning and more enjoyment of learning.

Teaching and learning adaptations

Many young people, especially those who struggle with learning, need a flexible response to be able to make the most of being in school. The first thing is to ask students what is most helpful to them. Most will be able to come up with their own ideas. Some pupils need more time to complete a piece of work, or the parameters of the task may be changed so that they achieve a section of it. This makes for depth rather than breadth but makes it more likely students will learn something rather than skim it. Scaffolding a task into smaller manageable steps also ensures that the pupil sees themselves making progress in their learning rather than attempting and failing at something out of reach. Some students also need more opportunities than others to practice something new until it becomes secure, and they can apply or generalise it. It may be useful to give some students prior information before introducing a new topic so they already have some knowledge when it is introduced to the rest of the class. This may include new words as well as new concepts.

Environmental adaptations

Some students will need a quieter, less distracting, place to sit in the classroom; others may need to be at the front. Pupils who do not feel secure in English may benefit from being with others who speak their language and can help translate.

When all students feel accepted and welcomed, whatever their backgrounds and needs, they will be more willing to engage. It is worth checking in with all pupils from time to time to see whether initial adaptations are still useful or need changing.

Citizenship in action

Citizenship is usually on the curriculum for secondary schools. The 'citizenship in action' component is defined as a planned course of informed action to address an issue or question of concern aimed at delivering a benefit or change for the community or wider society. It has the following aspects:

- Research and enquiry
- Interpretation of evidence (including primary and secondary sources)
- Planning
- Collaboration
- Problem-solving
- Advocacy and campaigning
- Evaluation.

All the above support aspects of learning across other disciplines. The percentage this contributes to the final mark for this subject has been downgraded in England from 60% to 15%. Therefore, it has been recommended that "*the scale of any action must be greatly reduced compared to previous practice*" (Pearson, 2023). Citizenship, however, may remain meaningless unless young people themselves experience what it means in action. This includes having a say in what concerns them. This aligns with Agency and also underpins the understanding that everyone has both a voice and a responsibility for ensuring that things are fair. This is the basis of a functioning democracy.

Student Representative Councils

Each class in the school is represented, preferably by two students. Individuals stand as candidates and say what is important to them and how they will represent the views of the class. Everyone has a confidential vote. The elected representatives meet regularly with the whole class to report on actions, seek information on what their fellow pupils wish to raise, and give opportunities to ask questions. The class could also elect two observers whose job it is to also attend Student Council meetings but without being able to vote.

The British Council has a UK Youth Parliament open to 11- to 18-year-olds, elected by their communities. Providing information on campaigns (at time of writing this was free school meals) may make active citizenship more relevant to the next generation.

Service-learning

Service-learning has many similarities to citizenship in action and is offered as part of education in many countries worldwide: not just volunteering, but students working with organisations to negotiate and plan intervention to effect change and become something greater than themselves. Service-learning has an academic component in addition to volunteering, such as a reflective journal, a call to action, and essays on what students have learned or accomplished. The interaction of knowledge and skills with experience deepens understanding. Students are often acknowledged for their contributions and demonstration of learning by formal accreditation recognised by institutions for both further and higher education.

Equity in practice across the secondary school

Strength through Diversity

The OECD's Strength through Diversity Project identifies the following six steps that incorporate what needs to happen at both a policy and practice level in schools to maximise Equity and Inclusion. The following is a summary:

- Policymakers need to question how education systems are governed, resourced and monitored to ensure they reflect the needs of *all* students.
- Funding models need to be designed with the explicit goal of fostering Equity and Inclusion. Regular and targeted funding should be balanced to avoid the multiplication of programmes, a lack of coordination and inefficiencies.
- Teachers and school leaders need Equity and Inclusion as core themes in initial and continuous professional learning. This fosters understanding how to address diversity in the classroom.
- All relevant stakeholders – students, parents, teacher unions, specific organisations – should be engaged to help promote equitable and inclusive policies. This will raise awareness of diversity issues, as well as create more positive classroom environments.
- Schools should identify and address the needs of students in each classroom. An Individual Education Plan can be developed and progress monitored. Schools can also support students through access to psychological services.
- Education systems need to be flexible and responsive to the needs of students. This can happen by providing different paths, such as academic and vocational choices; offering an inclusive curriculum; and adopting a range of teaching formats from one-on-one tuition to small group approaches.

Students with special educational needs and disabilities (SEND)

SEND education is about Equity, not equality, because education must be fair to every individual but it cannot always be the same.

(Paul Harris, 2019)

Where education systems are based on age rather than developmental needs, and teachers are expected to deliver a one-size-fits-all curriculum, inclusion in mainstream schools is inevitably more of a challenge for both pupils and educators. A rights-based approach to learning, however, says that students with additional needs have the right to be educated alongside their peers, including the right to make progress. This means creating the conditions that facilitate individual learning in an inclusive rather than segregated setting. Putting this into practice entails commitment, careful planning, close liaison with both families and professionals, professional learning for teachers, and flexibility. Although beliefs and perspectives are free, support can be expensive. Resource allocation is not always up to individual schools but dictated by the systems in which they are operating, so Equity can be elusive. It is not surprising that families often believe that they have to 'fight' for their children where funds are limited. Those who are more knowledgeable about how systems work, and have the resources to pay for professional support, are at an advantage in a competitive environment, entrenching further inequalities.

There have been university faculties devoted to inclusion for pupils with disabilities, and the issue is both complex and not without controversy. There are those, for instance, who reject the term 'special' needs, saying that everyone has needs that require meeting in different ways. The social model of disability differs from the medical model in saying that people are disabled by their environment and that once provision is in place they can have many of the opportunities offered to others. This is powerfully illustrated by issues of access.

Access

If you have ever needed to use a wheelchair you will know that there are places you cannot go, things you cannot do and experiences you cannot have because there is no provision for someone in a wheelchair. The need for adaptation to the environment applies to anyone who is otherwise unable to participate in what is on offer for everyone else. In a school this means enabling access to a full learning experience for everyone. Some enablers will entail cost but many will be simply doing things differently.

In Australia the Human Rights Commission list 31 ways in which students might be disabled and denied full access to education and what might help (see Resources at the end of the chapter). The attitudes and beliefs of educators as well as policymakers are critical.

According to the Disabled Living Foundation, there are 800,000 pupils in the UK with a disability, and the majority attend mainstream schools. Under the *Equality Act 2010*, all schools in the UK are required to have an accessibility plan. Following an access audit, this plan should include how the school aims to

- Increase the extent to which pupils with disabilities can participate in the curriculum
- Improve the physical environment to enable pupils with disabilities to take better advantage of the education, benefits, facilities and services provided
- Improve the availability of accessible information – not just in writing but using one or more other formats.

This is not just about buildings and books but asking pupils (and their families) what they need and what works for them. A one-size-fits-all approach is not applicable to special needs any more than it is to other young people.

Inclusive Design

Inclusive design, usually considered in relation to the built environment, places people at the heart of the process, acknowledges human diversity and offers dignity, autonomy and choice.

The principles are based on the social model where the 'problem' is not disabled people themselves but that individuals are made disabled by their environment, people's attitudes, policies and procedures.

Physical and some other disabilities are visible. Sometimes this can lead to exclusion or bullying but can also result in well-intentioned actions when the person is seen in the light of their disability and what they can't do, rather than a focus on the whole person and enabling adaptations that build independence. There are also hidden disabilities which may be harder to spot but also need flexible arrangements.

It is not just a small minority that need adaptations to access the learning environment. Acoustics, for instance, are not only an issue for those with limited hearing but also for those with poor sight who rely on sound. Neurodiverse students may find noisy environments overwhelming.

These are just a few of the material adaptations needed in schools: there are many more:

- Step-free or level access, with consideration also given to rugs, surfaces etc.
- Assistive listening systems
- Interactive white boards with colours such as pink on dark blue, which are more comfortable to read than black on white.

Young people just want to fit in, to join in if they want to, and as far as possible to be treated the same as everyone else. There is much that can be done to make this happen, but it takes an enabling perspective and a belief that it is worthwhile – not only for that individual in the here and now but also for the possibilities for their future.

Teresa Rumble, Senior Access Advisor and Inclusive Design Specialist, Centre for Accessible Environments, UK

As well as material adaptations, the knowledge and practices of educators are critical. The following provision, although not mainstream, has an approach to education that positions students and their potential in ways that are qualitatively different to many settings.

Doing Things Differently at Spaghetti Bridge

Spaghetti Bridge was founded with a clear and ambitious intention: to change the world through providing pupils with an environment and community in which they feel safe and that they matter, an educational programme tailored to their individual needs, and a curriculum and pedagogy that allow them to be active participants in their learning through a practical, project-based approach. We call this Enterprise Learning.

All Spaghetti Bridge students have an Education, Health and Care Plan which in the UK indicates a high level of educational need. The majority of their recognised needs fall into the area of social, emotional, and mental health, but many also have sensory processing and communication needs. Although the school is registered to work with six- to nineteen-year-olds, the majority are over twelve. Many have had a negative experience of education and lost confidence in their ability to learn, often to the extent that they are unable to attend a traditional school setting. To enable our students to reimagine their ability to learn, we have created our Three Phase Curriculum, which scaffolds their experience to challenge them to thrive and achieve their full potential.

The first stage of the Three Phases, 'Overcoming Barriers', begins with our Relational Approach, fostering a sense of connection and belonging, which lays the groundwork for the broader curriculum in the second stage, '21st Century Skills', in which they are further challenged to engage with a wider range of topics and subjects. Our third phase, 'Becoming Community Ready', provides students with the pathway that enables them to succeed beyond the school environment.

This 'difference-not-deficit' and 'stage-not-age' approach allows us to personalise education and to integrate our relational and academic curriculum, focusing on the skills, knowledge, and understandings that will foster students' development as holistic individuals. Projects and real-world experiences are the vehicle through which our students learn to relate to and cooperate with others, learn about the world through our Subject Pillars, and actively create new knowledge and broader understandings of the world through our Learning Cycle.

We have seen that by treating our students as active subjects in their education, they in turn rethink their potential to learn and be an engaged participant in and contributor to the world of the 21st century.

Christopher Lore, Group Head of Curriculum and Research Spaghetti Bridge School

To limit stereotyping, all pupils need awareness of people with a range of disabilities in a wide variety of roles. These include politicians, comedians, actors, scientists, academics, entrepreneurs and educators. The increased focus on the Paralympics in the last 20 years or so, as well as actors with disability being more visible, has given everyone a less restricted perspective. However 'normality' is defined, it should not be the only criterion for inclusion and success.

Outside spaces

Both greener views and surroundings, as well as time spent within green spaces, offer children numerous mental, physical and social developmental benefits and spur their growth into ecologically aware and responsible citizens. Moreover, when equally accessible, green spaces serve to reduce the health inequities suffered by socio-economically disadvantaged children.

(UNICEF, 2021)

There is now a wealth of research (Burke et al., 2023; UNICEF, 2021) that confirms that wellbeing is enhanced by being in nature – in the open air in green and blue spaces. In some communities there is little by way of open space at all, so it makes sense for schools, wherever possible, to arrange for pupils to visit parks, woods, countryside and seaside places and if that is not possible to find areas within the grounds where students can experience the natural world. Amongst other things, UNICEF suggests that schools

- Preserve, improve, create and maintain safe and accessible green spaces
- Integrate environmental education into the curriculum so that young people understand how important it is to take care of the natural world
- Set aside time for students to be outdoors during the day.

Creativity

An overwhelming focus on core subjects in the UK, alongside funding cuts to education in state schools, has led to what some have called a 'creativity crisis'. Other countries are also experiencing this. Activities such as art, music, dance and drama are often the highlight of the week for adolescents, but there is limited opportunity for students to engage in such subjects unless they are in independent schools. This means that careers in the arts are increasingly restricted to the privileged echelons of society.

Creative subjects matter for many reasons. For individuals, they allow for personal expression which may not have an outlet elsewhere. They provide a space for non-academic strengths to develop. This can motivate students to attend school, engage with learning and become more confident overall. They promote positive emotions that enhance wellbeing. When creativity is collaborative, this can build positive relationships and increase pro-social behaviour. Arts projects, such as putting on a performance, require planning, hard work and practice – skills highly valued by employers. Creative subjects enhance imagination, a skill at the heart of innovation, needed for the challenges of the 21st century. The creative industries are also among the fastest-growing economic sectors in the UK.

For future societies to thrive we need well-rounded citizens who can contribute to and enjoy wide cultural interests. School leaders may believe they do not have either the time or the resources for creative subjects, but time is finite – it is what is prioritised that matters. Although not the rich experience provided by taking arts subjects there are many ways to enhance creativity within classes and across a school. There are resources to help with this, such as the National Theatre Collection, free for all state schools (see Resources). Teachers sharing ideas with colleagues, giving students opportunities to explore options, and perhaps seeking community support, may enable more individuals to engage with creative activities – until they are again valued as central to a fair and vibrant education for all.

Behaviour

Loss

One secondary school was in the news several years ago for their much-lauded zero-tolerance policy and the 'improved discipline' they perceived as a result. One of the students excluded for their behaviour was a boy whose twin brother had been killed in a car accident the previous Christmas. In school, a sudden deterioration in pupil behaviour or reduced focus on learning is often an indication that something is happening that is distressing them. This might be a bereavement or family breakdown or perhaps where a parent has been imprisoned. A sensitive conversation with a parent, asking for their insights, may be a first step. Letting the student know you are aware that things are tough for them at the moment but that some behaviours are still not acceptable is one way of handling difficulties. It is also a good idea to have as much normal routine as possible, so that something in the young person's life is stable and reliable. Teachers do more than they know to provide a predictable and safe environment.

A valuable intervention is 'Seasons for Growth' (see Resources): this is an intervention peer support program for young people up to the age of 18. It is based on the belief that change, loss and grief are normal and valuable parts of life and is for any pupil who is dealing with major changes in their lives. The programme consists of eight weekly sessions of 50 minutes duration, led by a trained group facilitator (a 'companion') followed by a celebration session and two re-connector sessions. Using a Seasons metaphor to discuss change and growth, the group engages in games, discussion and creative activities. This helps young people connect with others and reduce feelings of isolation, understand the process of grief and develop coping strategies.

Trauma

Many students live in stressful situations, but this is different from trauma, which experiences outside normality that are overwhelming. They can result in hypervigilance, inability to sleep, flashbacks, terror, deep depression, helplessness and the need to re-assert control. Trauma experiences include family and community violence, serious accidents, physical and sexual abuse, refugee experiences, involvement in natural or climate crisis disasters, and witnessing scenes of inhumanity. Teenagers may also be profoundly affected by world events reported on the news. Adolescents who have experienced trauma may exhibit behaviour that is hard to manage. Some have low tolerance of frustration and exhibit irritation or aggression, while others withdraw and/or regress. They may look to peers for support rather than adults or family members. Sanctions for unwanted behaviour are meaningless for these students. Highly charged emotional distress can be triggered by sights, sounds, smells, anniversaries or anything else that brings back memories of the trauma. When a young person is overwhelmed and exhibiting a lack of control, trauma-informed responses include the following:

- Keeping a physical distance so as not to reinforce potential threat
- Acknowledging and validating the emotions being expressed
- Refocusing the student into the here and now
- Reassuring them they are safe
- Reminding them of their support networks
- Offering comfort and a safe, calm place of refuge

Identifying and removing potential triggers may reduce future incidents. A trusting relationship is the basis of effective intervention, but all educators need training and support when they have traumatised students in their care (see Chapter 5 on Respect).

Equity in the staffroom

There is a wealth of information about Equity in the classroom, but little that addresses the same or similar issues in the staffroom. There is more gender Equity than there was, but women are still vulnerable to institutional discrepancies. Although 74% of teachers in state schools are women only 65% of heads are female. In the UK in 2021 over 85% of all teachers in state schools were white middle class. This is unlikely to be overt discrimination but a subtle and more covert aspect of a historically embedded culture. People in these schools may be reluctant to challenge prejudice for fear this might generate conflict.

Performance-related pay is a danger to Equity. It is usually a reward for students achieving high scores on tests. This puts value on only one aspect of a teacher's role and has the potential to create a toxic culture.

Moving on

Assessment

The meaning of school in some countries has become increasingly focused on the attainment of high academic grades, often assessed in a single test that largely depends on the ability of the student to have good 'exam technique', retain information in the short term, and write this down on demand. Exams are usually a summative assessment – what a student knows on a certain day and time. An individual's performance might be affected by many things, including their health, family issues and levels of anxiety. For young people who have much to deal with, basing their final marks on end-of-year exams is fundamentally unfair and inflexible. Rather than acknowledging and celebrating accomplishments throughout education for everyone, it relegates a significant proportion of students as 'failures' or 'low achievers'. Many may go into key-worker roles, believing themselves to be less worthy than others – with pay and working conditions that reflect this.

The exam system and the resulting narrow curriculum are not only not meeting the needs of many young people but also not giving employers good information about potential employees or addressing the needs of business, such as team-building skills, critical thinking, creative innovation or good communications. In the UK, 89% of businesses believe it is important that young people be assessed on more than academic competence (cited in the Times Education Commission Report). It is now accepted in many quarters that we need to structure learning differently and be more flexible with assessing students' knowledge and capabilities. This is not only for the benefit of disadvantaged students but for everyone.

Alternatives for assessment

What is chosen will depend on what is being evaluated. These are just a few possibilities: some may be dependent on teacher judgment, but this is no less reliable than external examiners. Multiple assessment methods as in triangulated research may overcome bias.

- Basic knowledge – multiple-choice questions
- The ability to apply knowledge – demonstrating links with practice
- Deeper understanding of concepts – reflective journals, podcasts, presentations
- Research ability – answering questions with access to evidence online
- Insight and contribution to problem-solving – collaborative presentations
- The development of learning – portfolios of work over time
- Personal and interpersonal development: identification and demonstration of qualities and strengths – self and peer evaluation alongside teacher observation
- Attaining and retaining specific skills – measured against specific criteria that are either demonstrated and/or observed
- The ability to communicate knowledge and show how this might be generalised has a wide variety of potential assessment vehicles – written, oral and graphic.

Formative assessment

Continuous evaluation of a student's progress allows individuals to reflect on what is going well and what needs attention. When students see the incremental progress they are making, they are more likely to be motivated and engaged.

The International Baccalaureate

There are over 5,000 schools, with nearly two million students, who have adopted the International Baccalaureate as a framework for both curriculum and assessment. It is recognised across the world as a way of empowering school-age students to take ownership of their learning. It is broader than many other curricula and is focused on benefits to the whole community. The Times Education Commission Report recommends the development of a British Baccalaureate.

Further and Higher Education

Going to university and getting a degree is a pathway to a profession, often with status and eventual high salary. The better a student's exam grades, the greater their chance of securing a university place. The prevalence of this model means that students from well-heeled homes or private education have a better chance of securing the place of their choice. Those from disadvantaged backgrounds are often denied this opportunity, maintaining social and economic inequality. IntoUniversity has been established to address this.

Technical and vocational education and apprenticeships are often regarded in the UK as the Cinderella of post-school options, but there are indications that this is changing. A YouGov poll found that 44% of parents would prefer that their child study for an apprenticeship than an academic degree. Further education is also valued by countries, such as Singapore, that fully appreciate the rapidly changing world we are living in and fund a wide range of courses, not just for school-leavers but for those already in work who need to upgrade. According to the CBI (Confederation of Business Industry) in the UK 9 out of 10 people will need to reskill by 2030.

IntoUniversity

IntoUniversity aims to tackle educational inequality by creating home-from-home positive learning environments in which students facing disadvantage can rely on tailored additional support through their educational journey, as well as opportunities to build skills and knowledge. This is a long-term, multi-intervention programme supporting young people throughout school and beyond.

Our programme for secondary students

IntoUniversity provides a programme of specific support for Primary and Secondary students, meaning that, at secondary age, many students will already have had engagement with the organisation through primary programmes which begin from the age of 7, supporting academic development and conversations to start students thinking about their futures. Secondary students continue their work with **Into**University until they finish school. Weekly Academic Support continues but is more student-led than reliant on a structured curriculum. Students also receive support around things like work experience, university applications and CV-building. Secondary students have the opportunity to be paired with university students and corporate mentors to further support them.

Measuring success

At **Into**University, we believe every young person should be given the opportunity to reach their full potential, and to leave school with both the capability and confidence to make informed choices about their futures. Students who finish school after taking part in the programme are tangibly more likely to attend Higher Education than those from similar backgrounds who have not, and report improved grades.

- 61% of 2023 school leavers progressed to Higher Education compared to 28% of students from similar backgrounds nationally.
- 62% of Academic Support students report improved grades.

Many of these students have been attending **Into**University since they were in primary school, and have experienced the full range of support the charity offers throughout their school journey.

*   **Into**University *isn't just about getting into University but about beating the odds and managing the unpredictable and often unequal circumstances so many of us find ourselves in. (Harlem, 22-year old Reception Teacher & former IntoUniversity student)*

Adam Rahman, IntoUniversity Bristol East

For individuals and society to thrive we need to value and nurture the potential of all young people.

Giving learners greater capacity and flexibility to determine their educational pathways according to their evolving contexts, interests and needs gives them the best chance of reaching their potential – maximising opportunity and therefore enhancing equity. This may require education systems to become much more dynamic in the face of the short- and long-term economic and societal challenges.

(OECD)

Equity in social and emotional learning (SEL)

Equity in Circle Solutions is achieved by everyone having the opportunity for a turn, even if they choose to 'pass'. No-one is singled out. Over time, louder individuals become quieter and quieter students gain confidence. The teacher also joins in with all the activities, providing a good model of expectations and equity in learning.

Activities in SEL

Strengths in Circles Cards

There are seven statements for each of the six ASPIRE principles.
   These are four of those for Equity:

* We are strong together.
* We stand up for what is fair.
* We are equals.
* We can all participate.

In groups of three or four, students are given one of these statements and discuss the following questions together.

– What does this mean?
– What would it make people feel about being in this school?
– Is it already happening – how do we know?
– What else might we do?

Each group decides on one action. They give a brief report back to the Circle, emphasising the action. What they all agree on is put on display as a reminder.

Confidence Cake

Confidence is what people need to have a go, to speak out, and to not give up when they make a mistake.

In groups of three or four students are given a large piece of paper and coloured pens. They are asked to think of ingredients that would be needed for a 'confidence cake'. How would they mix these ingredients and what would be needed to make sure it was 'cooked'. Then how might they decorate it? After discussion they draw the finished cake and write the recipe using amounts, such as "*start with a kilo of ... add a big handful of ... a spoonful of ... and a sprinkling of ...*", etc. The finished 'cakes' are put on display. Students can be surprisingly creative and thoughtful in this activity.

Future Communities Collages

In groups of three or four students are given a piece of art board and a large variety of collage materials, scissors, glue, pens, newspapers, magazines and postcards. They are asked to think about the world they want for their future. What is important to them and their communities, how would people treat each other, what opportunities would there be, and what would bring joy into their lives? After the discussion, they create their collage with words, drawings and pictures. Each group has the opportunity to showcase what they have created, and the teacher points out similarities between them.

Group Dynamics

This activity raises awareness of what might happen in a group discussion. It is probably better to do this with one group in the centre of the Circle with others being asked to observe and then comment on what happens. Six students volunteer to be part of a group discussion to talk about an end-of-term event.

They sit on chairs in the middle of the Circle, and then each has one of the following sticky labels placed on their forehead. You may like to write the negative ones in red and the positive ones in green.

- – I am the leader.
- – Ignore me.
- – Build on my ideas.
- – Disagree with me.
- – Interrupt me.
- – Ask me questions.

The group are given five minutes to come up with a draft plan for their end-of-term event. Then each of the group is asked to say how it went and how they feel. They are asked if they can guess what was written on their forehead.

The rest of the Circle are asked to reflect on what they observed and to give feedback. In the following Circle everyone works in groups of six to do the same activity, this time being aware of the group dynamic.

Equity checklist

	This is in place - we know it is effective because …	Working on it – our actions to date are…	Just started - our next step will be…
All staff believe that every student can learn and has potential.			
All staff believe that every child has a right to education.			
Policies and practices acknowledge the need for flexibility.			
Policies and practices respect the need for fairness.			
Collaboration is encouraged.			
Staff have access to professional development on meeting the needs of diverse learners.			
Community action/ citizenship education is part of the curriculum.			
The school and learning are accessible to all.			

Equity in the future

'Levelling up' has become a catch phrase that looks good in political manifestos but means nothing unless there is action to make this happen. We cannot talk about tax cuts and social equality in the same breath. Ensuring that all children have opportunities to flourish means funding state education so that all schools have the infrastructure they need to meet diverse needs.

Professor Richard Wilkinson, co-author of *The Spirit Level* (2010), asserts that greater social equality is the most important factor in ensuring people's wellbeing. In contrast to less equal rich countries, more equal rich countries have, for example

- higher levels of education
- more trust and community involvement
- greater social mobility
- more wellbeing among children
- lower levels of physical ill health
- lower levels of mental ill health
- less drug abuse
- lower rates of imprisonment
- less obesity
- less violence
- fewer teenage births.

Societies with a bigger gap between the rich and the poor present challenges for everyone, including the well-off. While greater equality yields the greatest benefits for the poor, the benefits extend to the majority of the population.

What we have learnt throughout this chapter is that current education policy in the UK does not meet the needs of many young people. Some have chronic disadvantage, while others have issues in their lives which impact on their learning or behaviour at a given time. Giving learners greater capacity and flexibility to determine their educational pathways according to their evolving contexts, interests and needs, gives them the best chance of reaching their potential – maximising opportunity and therefore enhancing Equity. This may require education systems to become more dynamic in the face of economic and societal challenges.

For a nation to thrive and for the future to be secure so that everyone has the best chance to live life well, we need to change direction from focusing on what is good just for *me* to what is better for *us*.

References, further reading and resources

Armstrong, P.W., Brown, C. & Chapman, C.J. (2021). School-to-school collaboration in England: A configurative review of the empirical evidence. *Review of Education*, *9*, 319–351.

Bronfenbrenner, U. (1979). *The Ecology of Human Development: Experiences by Nature and Design*. Harvard University Press.

Brunzell, T. & Norrish, J. (2021). *Creating Trauma-Informed, Strengths-Based Classrooms. Teacher Strategies for Nurturing Students Healing, Growth and Learning*. Jessica Kingsley.

Burke, J., Clarke, D., O'Keeffe, J. & Meehan, T. (2023). The impact of blue and green spaces on wellbeing: A review of reviews through a positive psychology lens. *Journal of Happiness and Health*, *3*(2), 93–108.

Cattan. S., Contil, G., Farquaharson, C., Ginja, R. & Pecher, M. (2021). *The Health Impacts of Sure Start*. The Institute of Fiscal Studies. ifs.org.uk/publications/health-impacts-sure-start

Children's Society (2023). *Facts about young carers.* childrenssociety.org.uk/what-we-do/our-work/supporting-young-carers/facts-about-young-carers

Education Endowment Foundation (2017). Dialogic teaching: Evaluation report and executive summary. d2tic4wvo1iusb.cloudfront.net/documents/projects/Dialogic_Teaching_Evaluation_Report.pdf?v=1630925826

Gaheer, S. & Paull, G. (2016). *The Value for Money of Children's Centre Services: Evaluation of Children's Centres in England (Ecce) Strand 5.* Department for Education, Research Report.

Galtung, J. (1969). Violence, peace, and peace research. *Journal of Peace Research*, 6(3), 167–191.

Galtung, J. (1990). Cultural violence. *Journal of Peace Research*, 27(3), 291–305.

GovUK. (2023). gov.uk/government/collections/statistics-looked-after-children

Harris, P. (2019). SEND education should be about Equity, not equality. *Education executive*.

Kidd, D. (2020). *A Curriculum of Hope – As Rich in Humanity as in Knowledge.* Independent Thinking Press.

Lerner, M.J. (1980). *The Belief in a Just World: A Fundamental Delusion.* Springer.

Millard, W. & Menzies, L. (n.d.). The state of speaking in our schools. voice21.org/wp-content/uploads/2019/10/Voice-21-State-of-speaking-in-our-schools.pdf

OECD (2019). Fostering students' critical thinking and creativity: What it means in school. oecd.org/education/fostering-students-creativity-and-critical-thinking-62212c37-en.htm

Pearson Citizenship Studies (2023). qualifications.pearson.com/content/dam/pdf/GCSE/Citizenship%20Studies/2016/teaching-and-learning-materials/citizenship-action-guidance.pdf

Quinlan, D. & Roffey, S. (2021). Positive education with disadvantaged students. In M.L. Kern & M.L. Wehmeyer (Eds.), *The Palgrave Handbook of Positive Education.* Springer.

Sacker, M.E., Lacey, R. & Maughn, B. (2021). *The Lifelong Health and Wellbeing Trajectories of People Who Have Been in Care.* Nuffield Foundation.

Soller, A. (2001). Supporting social interaction in an intelligent collaborative learning system. *International Journal of Artificial Intelligence in Education*, 12, 40–62.

Sylvester, R. & Seldon, A. (Chairs) (2022). *Times Education Commission: Bringing out the best. How to transform education and unleash the potential of every child.* documentcloud.org/documents/22056664-times-education-commission-final-report

The Glossary of Education Reform (2016). edglossary.org

UNICEF Armenia (2021). *The necessity of urban green space for children's optimal development.* unicef.org/armenia/en/stories/necessity-urban-green-space-childrens-optimal-development

Voice21. (n.d.). voice21.org

Wilkinson, R. & Pickett, K. (2010). *The Spirit Level: Why Equality is Better for Everyone.* Penguin Books.

Other sources and further reading

Aynsley-Green, A. (2019). *The British Betrayal of Childhood: Challenging Uncomfortable Truths and Bringing out Change.* Routledge.

Beck, I. L., McKeown, M. G. & Kucan, L. (2013). *Bringing Words to Life: Robust Vocabulary Instruction.* Guildford.

Herrick, C. & Bell, K. (2022). Concepts, disciplines and politics: on 'structural violence' and the 'social determinants of health'. *Critical Public Health*, 32(3), 295–308.

Ivcevic, Z., Hoffmann J.D. & McGarry, J.A. (2022). Scaffolding positive creativity in secondary school students. *Educ. Sci.*, 12, 239.

Johnson, D.W. & Johnson, R.T. (2000). Cooperative learning, values and culturally plural classrooms. In M. Leicester, C. Modgil, & S. Modgil (Eds.), *Education, Culture and Values.* Falmer Press.

Krammer, S.M.S., Lashitew, A.A., Doh, J.P. & Bapuji, H. (2023). Income inequality, social cohesion, and crime against businesses: Evidence from a global sample of firms. *J Int Bus Stud*, 54, 385–400.

Lane, H.B. & Allen, S. (2010). The vocabulary-rich classroom: Modeling sophisticated word use to promote word consciousness and vocabulary growth. *The Reading Teacher*, 63(5), 362–370.

Leadsom, A. (2021). *The Best Start for Life: A Vision for the 1,001 Critical Days*. Early Years Healthy Development Review Report, Department of Health and Social Care.

NSPCC (2023). learning.nspcc.org.uk/children-and-families-at-risk/looked-after-children

OECD (2020). *Mapping policy approaches and practices for the inclusion of students with special education needs*. OECD Education Working Paper Number 227.

OECD (2020). *The impact of Covid-19 on student Equity and inclusion: Supporting vulnerable students during school closures and reopenings*. oecd.org/coronavirus/policy-responses/the-impact-of-covid-19-on-student-equity-and-inclusion-supporting-vulnerable-students-during-school-closures-and-school-re-openings-d593b5c8

OECD (2023). *Equity and Inclusion in Education: finding strength through diversity*. oecdedutoday. com/equity-and-inclusion-in-education

Riley, A. (2012). Exploring the effects of the 'Seasons for Growth' intervention for pupils experiencing change and loss. *Educational and Child Psychology, 29*(3), 38–53.

Rose, R. (Ed) (2010). *Confronting Obstacles to Inclusion: International Responses to Developing Inclusive Education*. Routledge.

Villanueva, K., Badland, H., Hooper, P., Javad, M.K., Mavoa, S., Davern, M., Roberts, R., Goldfeld, S. & Giles-Corti, B. (2015). Developing indicators of public open space to promote health and wellbeing in communities. *Applied Geography, 57*, 112–119.

Weigart, K.M. (2008). Structural violence. In L.R. Kurtz (Ed.), *Encyclopaedia of Violence, Peace and Conflict*. Elsevier.

Williams, J., Pollard, E., Cook, J. & Byford, M. (2022). Enhancing creative education. pec.ac.uk/ research-reports/enhancing-creative-education

Resources

OECD: *Equity in education: The foundation for a more resilient future*. oecd.org/stories/ education-equity

CASCAID: *What is Equity in Education and Why Does it Matter?* cascaid.co.uk/article/equity-in-education

Equity for Children: equityforchildren.org

Education Endowment Foundation – established to break the link between family income and educational achievement. UK

- educationendowmentfoundation.org.uk/education-evidence/guidance-reports/literacy-ks3-ks4
- educationendowmentfoundation.org.uk/education-evidence/secondary

dyscalculia.org/learning-disabilities/dysgraphia/writing-alternatives

Voice 21 is the UK's oracy education charity. voice21.org

sec-ed.co.uk/content/best-practice/quick-wins-for-teaching-oracy-skills

Seasons for Growth: an early intervention program to help children through grief, loss and major changes in their lives. seasonsforgrowth.co.uk

Hidden from View: The experiences of young carers in England childrenssociety.org.uk/sites/ default/files/2020-10/hidden_from_view_final.pdf

carers.org/how-your-school-can-support-young-carers/young-carers-in-schools

Stories of disabled people and their fight for Equity and access: wearealldisabled.org

Lifting Limits: this organisation works with schools to challenge gender stereotypes: liftinglimits. org.uk

The African-Caribbean Achievement Project, acap.org.uk

edutopia.org/article/teaching-critical-thinking-middle-high-school

my.chartered.college/impact_article/how-to-teach-critical-thinking

philosophy-foundation.org/stories-for-thinking

o-operation.org/what-is-cooperative-learning

byc.org.uk/uk/uk-youth-parliament

oxfam.org.uk/education/who-we-are/what-is-global-citizenship

edutopia.org/article/benefits-service-learning-high-school-students

National Theatre Collection: nationaltheatre.org.uk/learn-explore/schools/national-theatre-collection

Edutopia.org/creativity

The International Baccalaureate ibo.org

Roffey, S. (2020). *Circle Solutions for Student Wellbeing* (Sage) has an assessment module for 12 dimensions of social and emotional learning for years 2, 6, 9 and 12.

7 ASPIRE in action across the world

This final chapter illustrates the application of all of the ASPIRE principles (Agency, Safety, Positivity, Inclusion, Respect, and Equity) in educational settings across the world, and the impact this has on learning, wellbeing and school culture. Although there are vibrant examples of each principle throughout the book, it is when they are all threaded through everything that happens across the school community that sustainable change happens. This not only impacts the learning and wellbeing of students but also the wellbeing and efficacy of teachers. There are indications that ASPIRE also promotes positive engagement with the wider community. Step by step, we are beginning to create a brighter world.

School leaders and their vision for education

Positive education begins with a vision that encompasses the whole learner in every aspect of their development and every individual regardless of their ability, background or need. It is concerned with wellbeing as well as learning and how that learning takes place. Positive education also addresses school culture, how teachers feel about their profession, its challenges and rewards, and whether families and diverse communities also feel they belong.

It is school leaders who have the most influence as change agents in a school. They need to be able to communicate their vision clearly and succinctly in ways which enable the whole community to believe in these values and this way of being. Having credibility and behaving in alignment with their vision help school leaders to do this successfully. There will always be dissenting voices which need to be acknowledged and respected, but conversations change culture and once this reaches a critical point and people can see for themselves the positive differences being experienced, people will either get on board or leave.

As you read through the following case study you will find all the ASPIRE principles in action in both policy and practice.

Love: Learn: Lead

Ben Davis is the headteacher at St Ambrose Barlow Roman Catholic High School in Swinton, part of the city of Salford, near Manchester. The school population of 1100 students is mixed, with increasing cultural diversity and young people living in worsening economic circumstances, some experiencing severe deprivation. Despite this the school has attendance well above the national average, exam results are better than most local schools in the area, and teacher retention is good.

Twice a week in staff briefings Ben goes through the same slides that underpin the collective vision for his school. This reinforces the values that determine how things happen every day.

DOI: 10.4324/9781003428244-8

These are Love, Learn and Lead.

Love: This is defined as ensuring that everyone is safe, healthy and included. Positive relationships are at the heart of the school, and respect for human dignity is at the forefront of how people are expected to treat each other. This is inclusive of staff, students and the wider community. It is reflected in staff roles and responsibilities, such as the head of behaviour and attendance also being the head of relationships.

There are systems in place for recognising and celebrating students. Form teachers and students identify those to be awarded badges for demonstrating strengths such as kindness, respect, courage and creativity. Every Friday 42 students, the 'stars of the week' are invited to have mugs of hot chocolate in the canteen, something even older pupils enjoy. There is awareness amongst staff that words matter. Senior staff model this, such as greeting a border-line attender with warmth, '*Hi, great to see you, so pleased you are here*'. Young people not only attend but come back to see staff when they have left, especially more vulnerable pupils such as those who have been in care.

Teachers' work and effort are also recognised. A birthday card for each member of staff and scheduled 1-2-1 meetings with the Head for all staff throughout the year ensure they are respected and cared for in the school. Teachers considering leaving the profession have come to Ambrose Barlow and stayed.

Learn: The school wants everyone to achieve in ways that has meaning for them, both in and beyond school. This is not just about passing exams to demonstrate curricular knowledge and skills but learning wisdom – understanding at a deeper level in ways that will impact lives and relationships. The school was built without a library, so, with the help of the Director of Finance who applied for funding, they have built their own, enhancing not only academic learning for all but also the understanding that will and determination can change things. As is often the case in schools there are students with adverse childhood experiences and whose behaviour reflects this. Staff are trained in attachment theory, solution-focused coaching and trauma-informed education. Their own learning is as important as those they teach.

Lead: Although not everyone is a leader, Ben and his team believe that everyone should be able to lead a life that is meaningful for them. Students are asked what works for them, especially if they are more vulnerable. One neurodiverse student was asked what would make him feel safe in school. He was clear that, amongst other things, he needed to wear ear defenders because loud noises made him anxious, he couldn't wear the school uniform for sensory reasons, and he identified a member of staff with whom he felt particularly safe. Because the focus is on positive relationships, student voice is evident in every interaction. Everyone is involved in decisions made by the student council. One of these was the establishment of a one-way system in corridors to reduce chaotic transitions. This student initiative no longer needs adult supervision.

A simple message throughout the school is that "*everybody matters*". Ben tells students that although he is the Head, he does not matter more than anyone else.

Challenges: Schools are complex places and Ben is well aware that not everyone will embrace his vision. There are dissenting voices, not least in those who make policy and may judge schools on narrow performance measures. This can put pressure to focus on things other than what is in a student's best interests. "*Although we need to help kids pass exams,*" says Ben, "*the core business of my school is child development*". Equity is discussed all the time in St Ambrose, but removing barriers to education for many students is hard to achieve. Another major challenge is the cost-of-living crisis. Poverty not only impacts resources for the school, making inclusion harder, but also affects how students are living. Some are in mould-infested homes, others in families without access to basic needs. Staff liaise with many multi-agency partners to support where they can.

Hopes: This can be summarised as an education system fit for purpose for all young people, underpinned by a strong consensus about child development. Ben is already taking a lead in this by taking part, with others, to campaign for a fairer, safer and kinder system where every child can thrive and learn.

With thanks to Ben Davis

Although the following is an example from a primary school rather than secondary, it emphasises the power of the positive and walking the talk, aspects that apply in all educational settings.

Building a positive school culture in Australia

I first met Jason Miezis when doing research in Australia on what was involved in creating an 'emotionally literate school'. He was the then principal of Rouse Hill Public School, and his focus on the positive was in evidence everywhere. A laminated poster announcing 'This is a No Put Down Zone' was in every classroom, corridor, hall, the school office, principal's office and staff room. Pupils told me that they did not have bullying in their school, because "we've got this no put down thing". Teachers told me that Jason's positivity was infectious, and they clearly appreciated his approach because he walked the talk. While I was interviewing staff before school he was busy with a barbecue making them breakfast. Even staff who at first were cynical had come around to his way of thinking. Clearly it was having a positive impact on wellbeing for staff as well as students; the sickness budget for the school was regularly underspent – giving more options for professional development activities.

This is an excerpt from a newsletter where Jason was also principal:

We often refer to the term 'wellbeing' at our school. Wellbeing is a term used in all industries, but in an educational context, wellbeing centres on schools creating teaching and learning environments that enable students to be healthy, engaged and successful. The Department of Education has a Wellbeing Framework for Schools which provides teachers with a scaffold to ensure students' needs in the areas of cognitive, emotional, social, physical and spiritual wellbeing are maximised. We all want our students to be connected, successful and to thrive with their learning. At Cherrybrook Public School, the care, courtesy and love that teachers show for students is evident on a daily basis. I feel very proud to lead a team of delightful staff members who want students to thrive, flourish, do well and, as our school motto suggests, learn and grow.

With thanks to Jason Miezis, former principal of Rouse Hill and Cherrybrook Public Schools, New South Wales

Social and emotional learning (SEL)

Social and emotional learning is where learners think about who they want to become, the values that support their wellbeing, the relationships that enhance their lives, and the health of their communities and the planet. SEL is included in every chapter because this gives students opportunities to engage with the ASPIRE principles in a way that encourages discussion, reflection and sometimes action. It is not just what we teach that matters, however, but how we do it. Circle Solutions is a framework for SEL that incorporates the ASPIRE principles as a pedagogy to ensure that this is a safe, solution-focused, strengths-based space for both teachers and learners. Circle Solutions is not a stand-alone intervention but, as Lily Liu illustrates here, a tool for wellbeing across the school.

Circle Solutions in China

The Covid epidemic profoundly impacted mental health worldwide. As the principal of Dehong Chinese International School in Xi'an, I needed something to support social and emotional learning for all our students. Since 2020 we have used the principles and methods of Circle Solutions and incorporated these into our curriculum. I want to share the positive impact this has had on our school's students, teachers and administrators.

Circle Solutions helps our students establish positive connections, enhances their confidence, sense of belonging, and improves their social skills and self-awareness. They communicate their thoughts safely and avoid negative comments. They learn how to get along with others and express their ideas and emotions through different activities. In a warm, inclusive and safe atmosphere the children cherish this opportunity to communicate. In the Circle, teachers and students are on an equal footing which helps them understand each other, reduces isolation, promotes listening and appreciation of others.

In Circles, teachers are not only guides and listeners but participants and sharers. The traditional teacher-centred approach is replaced by an equal and trusting relationship, so teachers better understand their students and provide them with teaching content and methods that meet their needs and interests. Teachers also use weekly Circles to share their own experiences and get support and feedback from colleagues and managers.

Circle Solutions not only addresses students' social and emotional development, but also pays attention to teacher mental health. We have established a Wellbeing Centre in the school based on Circle Solutions principles where both Circle trainers and counsellors have helped to make the school more positive, inclusive, open-minded and innovative.

I have witnessed the huge changes Circle Solutions has brought to the school in the last three years. Our students are more confident, friendly and cooperative; our teachers more equal, trusting and professional; and our managers more empowering, supportive and innovative. By creating a friendly and harmonious atmosphere Circle Solutions has improved the wellbeing of the whole school.

Lily L.J. Lui, Principal, Dehong Chinese International School Xi'an

Building on what is working

Most schools are already using some or all of the ASPIRE principles in a myriad of different ways, often without fully realising this. It is valuable to appreciate what is already in place and working well, so that staff and students can explore ways to develop this.

Educational psychologists are often positioned as professionals who carry out assessments with children and recommend interventions. But a unitary focus on this role limits their potential to support educational change. They invariably have substantial knowledge on school systems, child development, behaviour, relationships, motivation, learning and wellbeing as well as skills in observation, communication and collaborative practices. Many are more than happy to work with schools pro-actively to develop effective ways of enhancing learning and wellbeing for all. This is just one example.

Educational Psychologists Supporting Schools with ASPIRE in England

Educational Psychologists (EPs) at Hampshire and Isle of Wight (IOW) Educational Psychology Service have been using the strengths-based ASPIRE framework to support schools' wellbeing practice.

The Strengths in Circles cards comprise 42 statements – seven for each of the ASPIRE principles. These show what these principles mean in practice, such as 'We are kind to each other' and 'We show gratitude'. The EPs shared these with Special Educational Needs Co-ordinators (SENCos) who then went together for a 'learning walk' around the school to look for evidence of each statement in practice. Notes were made and photos taken each time practice that illustrated one of the statements was identified. This was not just what was visible but also verbal interactions. As well as classrooms, we went around the building, including the reception area.

SENCos found the framework easy to understand and enjoyed the learning walk observations and sharing photos with the whole staff team, generating discussion on good practice across the school. One SENCo planned to share Strengths in Circles cards with pupils who could Blu-Tack them to things they saw which showed how the statement was true. This has helped staff understand how to support relationships and wellbeing in a respectful and empowering way.

An audit tool was created using the "We ..." statements under each heading of the ASPIRE framework. It is planned that this tool will be used by schools (with their EP) to audit each area of the framework by considering whether each statement is enhanced, established, developing, or not yet developing, listing examples of good practice and/or next steps depending on the level chosen. This audit tool has been shared with schools at a wellbeing conference run by Hampshire and IOW Educational Psychology and was well received.

Sam Cox and Anna Beasley, Educational Psychologists, Hampshire and Isle of Wight

---

Photographs taken by children are considered a valuable way to explore experiences in children's daily lives (Dockett et al., 2017).

Schools in context

Each person is both wonderfully unique but also part of our shared humanity, having things in common with others. So are schools! There is no one size fits all. People will have their own priorities, circumstances, needs and resources. This is illustrated by this initiative in South Africa, building wellbeing across six schools with the ASPIRE principles guiding the process and supporting sustainability.

The Franschhoek wellbeing initiative in South Africa

There is a small town situated in a beautiful valley in South Africa, where six school communities, both primary and secondary, comprising 4,000 learners, their parents, teachers and other staff members, pursue a shared vision to enhance the quality of life in the community. They are doing this through the implementation of a holistic wellbeing process. Each school has a wellbeing support team and a wellbeing coordinating committee functioning across the six schools, who have been overseeing the sustainability of the process for the past seven years. The members of the committee are often asked "*How is this possible?*" The answer to this sustainability question is the ASPIRE framework applied as a critical lens for reflecting on the process.

The implementation of the holistic school wellbeing process, enhances Agency of pupils, staff and parents by providing access to opportunities where they can voice needs and challenges, share ideas to promote health and wellbeing, address challenges, and learn to listen to one another. These opportunities involve small group discussion, WhatsApp group chats and feedback reports. During one of the discussion sessions conducted to get feedback on the process, a Grade 7 pupil to everyone's surprise confidently challenged the school principal about the discipline in the school, stating: "*Sir, if I may say, I do not agree with your viewpoint.*"

In the secondary schools, learners took the initiative in organizing their own wellbeing interventions. A student council member excellently explained the holistic wellbeing process to a group of stakeholders who visited the school. Teachers who initially questioned the process became advocates for the promotion of health and wellbeing. Unemployed parents started volunteering at the school with pride and confidence. In essence, members took agency for the promotion of health and wellbeing in their own contexts.

The physical and emotional Safety of learners is enhanced through interventions such as Kind Kids Month – during which kindness in various forms and across various levels of engagement has been enhanced. Just picture the ripple effect of 4,000 learners each wearing a KIND KIDS bracelet, designing posters to enhance kindness in their specific contexts. Concurrently, discussing challenges associated with unsafe spaces, to ensure that pupils and staff are in touch with the impact of unkind acts and the importance of practicing kindness every day. Annual workshops to prepare primary school Grade 7 pupils to access secondary school provide opportunities to address their fears. Collaboration with a non-profit organization which provides individual psycho-social support enables teachers to make sure that pupils in distress have a safe space to go.

The deliberate enhancement of Positivity as a way to challenge the negative mindset that focuses on problems rather than on assets and solutions gained ground as the process developed. A slow and sometimes lonely process for those who initially chose this road less travelled. Yet gradually more members noted the benefits of a positive take on life – pupils reporting that positive input from peers and teachers enhance their confidence; teachers acknowledged that they have a new and more grateful perspective on life; parents understanding why supporting their children is an investment in the future. In the process, challenges became opportunities to find solutions together and building a more hopeful future. A Positive mindset clearly enhanced all relationships across the schools, as they introduced teacher and parents' appreciation days. Members across all levels started to appreciate one another's role in their school communities.

The appreciation and joy associated with being Included unconditionally, irrespective of role, status or academic achievement, to participate in the holistic wellbeing process. Amazing stories of: visiting places never seen before due to socio-economic challenges; broadened horizons through personal development workshops for secondary school learners, dress-up days for the primary school learners; facilitating participation in sport and cultural events in collaboration with non-profit organizations for more pupils; inviting parents to be part of family fun days over the weekend when they are available. The responses when pupils realise that there are no conditions for inclusion in this process, just a decision to participate, are priceless, especially for those pupils and parents who have always been looking on from the margins. The connectedness resulting from these cross-level engagements contributes to a positive school climate.

The emphasis on Respectful engagements as a basis for the promotion of health and wellbeing enhanced the recognition of every individual as a worthy member of the school community. Teachers admitted how their struggle to accept some parents and pupils based on their circumstances turned into understanding and care as lived values. Each member is seen as important and recognised as contributing to the holistic wellbeing process. Values are no longer simply displayed as words but lived through appreciative engagements, care, and a willingness to see the other as a fellow human being on which my wellbeing depend and whose wellbeing I impact – I am because you are.

The sound of Equity echoes through all the activities as the teams relentlessly work to keep as many members involved in the process, with the aim of enhancing the quality of life of each member to remove the barriers that might impact on their health and wellbeing. Each academic year starts with a motivational intervention – 'Future me' – to encourage all pupils to do their best. In this process power plays are challenged to ensure that the strength lies in the power of unity rather than power over others. Communication bridges are built across all levels of the system to open up ongoing conversations about moving closer to the shared vision. We are enhancing the quality of life in the community through the implementation of a holistic wellbeing process infused with the ASPIRE principles.

Prof Ansie Kitching, University of the Western Cape, South Africa

Sam and Anna identified different ways that schools were enacting ASPIRE, and Ansie has written about the myriad of actions supporting wellbeing and learning in what are often challenging circumstances. This is why this checklist below is not set in stone. What is likely to happen is that when people start paying serious (and playful!) attention to the context of wellbeing and learning in school, positive practice often snowballs.

ASPIRE checklist

	This is in place – we know it is effective because …	This is the impact on various stakeholders	This is how we might extend our practice	Working on it – our actions to date are …	Just started – our next step will be …
AGENCY					
SAFETY					
POSITIVITY					
INCLUSION					
RESPECT					
EQUITY					

And finally ...

What do students say about being in school – do they feel empowered, safe, enjoy learning, feel they belong and are respected? Do they believe that people genuinely care about their learning and wellbeing, and are they able to access what is on offer, develop their strengths and make progress? Do they wake up on a Monday morning looking forward to being in school?

What do teachers say about working in school? Do they feel empowered, safe and respected? Do they enjoy being there and feel supported and nourished? Do they have opportunities to face challenges, with help if necessary, and grow in their understanding and practice? Do they anticipate kindness and trust? Do they wake up on a Monday morning looking forward to the week ahead?

What do families and communities say about the school? Do they feel confident that the school has their child's best interests at heart? Do they feel safe about coming and talking to teachers about their concerns, and are there opportunities to ask questions and for clarification? Are their culture and context recognised and taken account of?

I went to a conference recently, and one of the presenters – a recent graduate – talked about her experiences in education. She used a phrase which surprised me. She talked about the need for 'radical love'. But when I thought about it, I came to the conclusion that this is the essence of ASPIRE. Each principle looks fairly simple and is in fact commonplace but when put into practice can be revolutionary. Not just a fleeting emotion or experience but a way of connecting the private and public sphere. What happens with individuals, with schools and in communities changes values, beliefs, relationships and priorities. This can, over time, change the world we live in now, the world our children will inherit, and the world our students and schools construct together. It can build hope.

Reference and further reading

Dockett, S., Einarsdottir, J., & Perry, B. (2017). Photo elicitation: reflecting on multiple sites of meaning. *International Journal of Early Years Education*, 25(3), 225–240.

Grenville-Cleave, B., Gudmundsdottir, D., Huppert, F., King, V., Roffey, D., Roffey, S, & de Vries, M. (2021). *Creating the World We Want to Live In: How Positive Psychology Can Build a Brighter Future*. Routledge.

Roffey, S. (2007). Transformation and emotional literacy: the role of school leaders in developing a caring community. *Leading and Managing*, 13(1), 16–30.

Sirkko, R., Kyrönlampi, T. & Puroila, A.M. (2019). Children's agency: Opportunities and constraints. *International Journal of Early Childhood*, 51, 283–300.

Index

Pages in *italics* refer to figures and pages in **bold** refer to tables.